Born to Win

BORN TO WIN

Woody Guthrie

EDITED BY **ROBERT SHELTON**

COLLIER BOOKS

Portions of this book are from the personal files of Moses Asch, Folkways Records, and Sing Out! magazine. The editor and publisher acknowledge and give thanks to these parties for permission to use this material.

Thanks also to Marjorie Mazia Guthrie and to countless friends of Woody Guthrie who have supplied the material that made this book possible.

First Collier Books Edition 1967
Second Printing 1970

Library of Congress catalog card number: 65–20187

The Macmillan Company
866 Third Avenue, New York, N.Y. 10022
Collier-Macmillan Canada Ltd., Toronto, Ontario

Born to Win was orginally published in a hardcover edition
by The Macmillan Company

Printed in the United States of America

The editor and publisher thank the trustees
of the Guthrie Children's Trust Fund—
Harold Leventhal, Peter Seeger and Lou Gordon—
for their cooperation and assistance
in the preparation of this book.

THIS BOOK IS DEDICATED TO THE MEMORY OF
Bill Rogers Guthrie
AND
Cathy Ann Guthrie
AND TO
Sue
Gwendolyn
Arlo
Joady
Nora

We hope they will see their world with the same zest and hopefulness.

Contents

Introduction

The facts of Woody Guthrie's life seem to say he was born to lose, but his belief that the underdog will eventually triumph has sustained him.

Born to Win is Woody's greatest testament of his faith in man. Despite a tragedy-stalked life, endured through the Depression and World War II, Guthrie never lost that faith, nor the powers of affirmation in the face of hardship.

The songs and ballads of Woody Guthrie have been growing in popularity for a decade, but only a few people have been aware of his literary worth. The publication of this collection of essays, prose poems, verse, journal notes, maxims, song lyrics, and letters will change all that. It takes no scholar to see in these writings the hand of a gifted folk poet, of a major American literary figure.

For here is a writer who embodies the Depression and the war years that followed. Here is a wry-witted word-volcano, a prophet singer, who was *there*—in the Dust Bowl exodus, with the migratory workers in the California orchards, with the assembly-line robots trying to become men in the union organizing drives, with the Negroes who sought dignity before the battle became a mass movement. Guthrie was there —on the trains, the highways, the torpedo-threatened merchant marine sea lanes.

Woody Guthrie wrote more than one thousand songs. Some are good, some ephemeral; many have become classics, part of the folk bloodstream of our country. He has been called "a rusty-voiced Homer" and "the greatest balladmaker America has ever known." His songs have entered the oral tradition of American literature: "Pastures of Plenty,"

"This Land Is Your Land," "Roll On, Columbia," "The Reuben James," "So Long, It's Been Good to Know You," "Tom Joad," "Dust Bowl Refugees," "Hard Traveling," "This Train Is Bound for Glory"—the list is as long as the freshet of words that poured from the writer from 1936 to 1952.

And the message of the songs and ballads is not distant from the message of this book. He is saying that words are magic gifts, that humans of all ages are inspired creatures, that there are people to love and some to fight—underdogs to love, and those who "steal with their fountain pens" and power, to fight.

Part of the Guthrie story has been told in his autobiography, *Bound for Glory*, published in 1943. He was born in the oil boomtown of Okemah, Oklahoma, in 1912. He went on the road at the age of 13, after his mother fell prey to Huntington's Chorea, the incurable degenerative nerve disease that has stilled his own voice and pen these past ten years.

In 1935, he joined the Dust Bowl refugees on their trek westward. For a time, he had a radio show for one dollar a day on WKVD in Los Angeles. With Will Geer, the actor, and the late Cisco Houston, the singer, he traveled to the migratory labor camps and helped raise some money for the workers there. His association with the late Mike Quin, columnist for *The People's Daily World*, has been said to have had a strong effect on Woody's writing and thinking. It was an era of radical problems and radical solutions.

After writing and distributing his mimeographed songbook, *On a Slow Train Through California*, he headed East. There he began his long friendship with Pete Seeger, the folk singer, and Alan Lomax, the folklorist who recorded him at length for The Library of Congress in 1940. Woody came to know the then pioneer folk-song world of New York— Burl Ives, Leadbelly, Josh White, Sonny Terry.

In 1941, Woody, Seeger, Lee Hays, and Millard Lampell started The Almanac Singers, touring the country from their home base in Greenwich Village. It was there, in the Village, that the first Manhattan hootenannies—the term borrowed from a Democratic Party benefit in Seattle—were held.

There were many times when Woody, individually or with other performers, might have made a handsome living as a commercial performer. Some saw in him another Will Rogers. But his inevitable refusal to compromise and his compulsively "itching heel," as Seeger has called it, kept Woody traveling away from the clutches of a "career" as a folk singer.

He did record "Dust Bowl Ballads" for Victor, and began to record adult and children's songs for Moe Asch on the Asch and Disc labels, forerunners of Folkways Records. There were three marriages and divorces and many children.

If the chronology becomes fuzzy, that's because Woody could say he was going to the corner for a pack of cigarettes and write from the West Coast three weeks later.

He was always writing. Recalls another singer-writer, Millard Lampell: "He had a marvelous sense of life and vitality. Woody would write all night . . . a news clipping would set him off for forty or fifty pages. He wrote some of the most breathtaking things I have ever read. . . . He was tormented, self-destructive, yet enormously fertile. He really believed in the power of music to make people alive."

To Cisco Houston, Woody was "the greatest folk poet we've had. He was like the Biblical prophets, who originally were men who sang the news." Cisco, who had "traveled by the side-door Pullman and the sun-burned thumb" with Woody, told me a few years ago that "anyone who knew a hard way of life would feel that Woody spoke for them. They identified with him."

Alan Lomax has called Guthrie "the best ballad-maker to come down the American 'pike, and in many ways the most truthful and most talented man of his generation."

We must look beyond the songs to find the full importance of Woody Guthrie. As a song-maker, he has earned the stature he deserves. But his reputation as a writer, poet and philosopher is still underground and must be brought into the light. When his songs, poems, and essays are studied in our American literature classes, this omission may be righted.

Woody Guthrie has been in the hospital since 1954. He is a wispy-haired, small-framed giant who appeared on the face of the American landscape, spreading hope and belief and a faith in the American democratic spirit. He was an inspired writer with a reverence for words and the people who gave him those words. Now, a part of that treasury of unpublished words is here for you to share.

RÓBERT SHELTON

N.B. Dates and places are provided for each piece wherever they are known. In most cases, the author's stylized spelling, punctuation and grammar have been retained. Like the nasal twang in his singing voice, he meant it that way.

Born to Win

People I Owe

. . . I think . . . back through my life to everybody that I owe, I mean, the ones I can remember in person. Of course, I know that I owe these folks, and that they owe some other people, these are in debt to others, and all of us owe everybody. The amount that we owe is all that we have.

And the only way that I can pay back all of you good walkers and talkers is to work, and let my work help you to get work, the kind of work you like best and can best perform. Your labor has already helped me, and it goes on helping me. I've got to know in a solid way that my work is helping you.

My work in these days is mainly writing. I write songs, ballads, stories with tunes, tales with no melody, wild lines with free beats and freer rhythms. These rhythms alone are as pretty as the paint on your tractor, the oil on your wheel, but I have painted your tractor, hoed lots of hard rows of weeds out of your cotton and out of your corn. I did not have the time to learn all there is to know about free rhyme and rhythm. I never did get quick enough to read the notes of music, nor to write them down. I never learned many of the upper laws of mathematics, nor high language.

But, I did keep my eyes on you, and kept my ears open when you came close to me. I saw the lines chopped across your face by the troubles in time and space. I saw the wind shape your face so the sun could light it up with thoughts and shadows. I remember your face as it was when I saw you. I hear your voice in its own loose words like it spoke when I heard it. I saw the several ways that your eyes got dark and light while you talked. I saw your hopes shine back in your eyes at times when you kept quiet.

And even when you kept quiet I could see your wants on your face, because you told me those wants and I made your wants a part of my wants. I told you my troubles and you made my troubles a part of your troubles. You told me the things you knew and I learned how to tell you what I know. You patted your hands while I danced, and held my head in your lap while I cried. But I am thirty-four now, and in these past few years I haven't cried much.

I guess I got to where the only way that I could cry was on some piece of paper in words like these. I have heard a storm of words in me, enough to write several hundred songs and that many books. I know that these words I hear are not my own private property.

I borrowed them from you, the same as I walked through the high winds and borrowed enough air to keep me moving. I borrowed enough to eat and drink to keep me alive. I borrowed the shirt you made, the coat you spun, the underwear you fixed, and those socks you wove. I went on and walked down my road, you went on and walked your path. And the weather's winds, snows, sleets, ices, and hailstones cut down the oat straw, beat through the car top, knocked holes in shingles and went through awnings, broke window lights, but never separated our works. Your works and my works held hands and our memories never did separate. I borrowed my life from the works of your life. I have felt your energy in me and seen mine move in you.

You may have been taught to call me by the name of a poet, but I am no more of a poet than you are. I am no more of a writer of songs than you are, no better singer. The only story that I have tried to write has been you. I never wrote a ballad nor a story neither one that told all there is to tell about you. You are the poet and your everyday talk is our best poem by our best poet. All I am is just sort of a clerk and climate tester, and my workshop is the sidewalk, your street, and your field, your highway, and your buildings. I am nothing more nor less than a photographer without a camera. So let me call you the poet and you the singer, because you will read this with more song in your voice than I will.

My wife and my friends read my pages as I write them, and they put more of the sound of poetry into the words than I ever do. It is you, the reader of the page, that catches the cannon breath and drum beat off the written page. I am no more, no less than your clerk that writes it down, like a debt always owed and partly paid. This book is a book of debt and part payment.

March 13, 1946
Coney Island

Your Word Singer

There'll be no sound of the give-up croaker in me,

No trap you set can bait me into a long heavy death talk.

I'll do every job I can to keep away from that deathy hole.

I'll do all I can to stay alive and argufying, alive and kicking, alive and flurking the dog.

I'll mozie and smooch around like a cheap detective and listen to you talk and watch you work,

And I'll take your words and use them not to rip you down, but to squeeze you up against the wall in ways that will put new life into your old pots and

Your old pans,

And new grease, honey, in your old washy dish rag.

[19]

I'll be a man, as best and worst and quick as I can.

A man as hot as I can.

And one day

You might even call me your word singer.

September 6, 1948

Folk Songs Are On Their Way In

I've heard several pretty smart thinkers tell me that folk songs are on their way out. That folk music as we hear it and know it is on its way out the old gate of history. That a folk song, to be called a folk song, must wear a snatch of hair and whiskers older than an oily leather skin drum.

They say that folk music and folk songs can't be clocked and timed, cut nor polished, whetted, whittled, nor ground down to fit into your highly artistic concerts and onto the grooves of our three-minute records for our nickel machines, radios, movies, dances, and keep up the sparks of natural and native fires which burn in the blood of all good folk songs and folk stories set to folk tunes.

I say that folk music and folk songs, folk ballads, are just now getting up onto their feet, like Joe Louis after a couple of sad knockdowns. Every other kind of an art that you can mention has been peeled about the jaw and eyes, mainly because you can't fill out any kind of a civil service paper and find a green government check in your mailbox for making up and playing folk music and folk songs. You've got to go to work down at a factory and spend two thirds of your time doing a job you hate in order to have enough money to go on with your folk songs and your folk music. You can toot your flute in a military band and get GI pay for it, you can slide your rod in a whoopyjive herd and get GI pay for that. But there's not any GI kale that you can lay a finger on to make up folk songs and folk music.

The best of marching I saw in my eight months in the army was to the folk words of a folky chant tune that went:

> Ain't no use in writin' home
> Some joker got your gal an' gone.
> Hey, boy, ya' got left, right?
> Ho, boy, ya' got right.
>
> Monkey an' a jay bird settin' onna fence
> Hey, boy, ya got left.
> Playin' 'em a chune onna monkey wrench
> Ho, Boy, ya got right.
>
> Ho, boy, Y' got left, right?
> Ho, boy, Y' got left?
> Ho, boy, Y' got left, right?
> Hey, man, Y' got left.

I went through four army camps in my short spell of it. Started at Fort Dix, N.J., on to Sheppard's Field, Texas, back up to Scott's Field, St. Louis, Illinois (with the boys) (an' a-gittin' my IQ's, interviews, movies, an' shots, my nickel beer, popcorn, an' back alley trots). I got a diploma to say that I was a teletype operator, and my last field was out there twenty some odd miles right in north of Las Vegas, Lost Wages, Nevada. I saw from fifty thousand to a hundred thousand men in every field, and not all of them could whistle the melody strain of any one classical piece, nor all sing the right words to any one popular jukebox number. I believe to my soul that every man in every camp could add on seven vulgar verses to the old marching yell, "Hey, Boy, Y' Got Left."

About sixteen years back down my road I started making up little songs, true stories, wild tales, long and short hauls about things I saw happen to the oil people, cattle people, wheat folks, on the upper north plains of high Texas, where the wind and the dust was born. I got onto a Pampa, Texas, radio station of six or eight watts, every morning, and I sung and played by myself and with other musicians around at outdoor platforms of parking lot beer joints. My dad and myself made up crazy songs just for the fun of it. "Flapper Fanny's Last Ride," "Barbary Ellen's Likker Pot," "Windy River Blues," "Dust Pneumonia," "Talkin' Dustbowl Blues," and all kinds of tall tales with the names of our kinfolks stuck in. If I didn't like my uncle that week, I'd make up a song where he would get shot, hung, swung up, and drowned. If you made me like you, I'd sing your name into a song where you struck out down the rock road feelin' sorta funny an' found a big pocketbook chuck full of money. I'd do these same things with the names of people well known around town and keep the airail waves posted with the latest gossip, news, and blues of the day. I kept this up for thirty minutes a day on Los Angeles radio station KFVD, telling and singing tall and windy tales with a labor move-ment slant, oh, for two years. I got more than twenty thou-sand handwritten letters from folks from Canda down to Tia Juana, desert rat prospectors, seamen on the Pacific boat-decks, snowy skiiers, Reno divorcers, as well as all of the trade union local halls up and down the westerly coastline. This was really where the first little lights dawned on me of what a folk poem, a folk tale, a folk ballad, a folk tune, really was. And my own original songs now have been on not just the three big radio dragnets, but I've been on most of their big and little programs in my flesh and on my fifteen albums of commercial records, both by the box and by the bulk. No. I've not got rich. I've made up scaddles and oodles of songs, ballads, about fires, floods, droughts, stabbings, rapings, killings, robbings, fist fights, gaming gamblers, riverboat rustlers, outlaws, inlaws, bad men, bad gals, wrecks of trains, cars, planes, ships, terrible accidents, political rally songs, songs of protest, trade union songs, ballads to tell you how racial hate's got another good man and gone, sugar loaf jumps to tell you how pretty you dive and swim, to tell you how I love you, hate you, need you, and can't stand you. I mix up old tunes, I wheel them and I deal them, and I shuffle them out across my barking board, I use half of two tunes, one third of three tunes, one tenth of ten tunes. I always save back my notes and words left over and pound them out to poke fun at the democrats and the republicans and these Wall Street ramblers.

My wife, Marjorie Mazia Guthrie, is now a dancer and a teacher of the modern dance around Martha Graham's studio, the Neighborhood Playhouse, the YMHA, and other scattered places. We made up twelve songs for the Disc Company of America (Moe Asch), called "Songs to Grow On" and "Work Songs to Grow On." We've already clipped and saved lots of reviews calling our kids' songs the best of the lot in the kids' record shops. We've put on several kids' parties with Marjorie herding the kids to the whangs of my mouth organ and guitar. Folks tell us everywhere we whirl and yell that they've never seen so many kids of all ages have so much fun before now. As long as I can slap my hands against my britches' legs and holler out how pretty Marjorie looks when she's dancing, folk songs are on their way in, not out. Just as long as Papa and Mama Bird sing for their newlycome babies, folk songs are still on their way in, not out. As long as we've got wrecks, disasters, cyclones, hurricanes, explosions, lynchings, trade union troubles, high prices and low pay, as long as we've got cops in uniform battling with union pickets on strike, folk songs and folk ballads are on their way in.

As long as a woman and a man walk off somewhere and fall in love with each other, talk, sing, hum, whistle, and dance around one another, folk songs will be on their way in. I thump my woodblock here and hum to myself, and I yell out this chorus ten jillion times, that, just as long as the folks are on their way in, the folk song will be on its way in.

Me and the Others

You know when I think about me and the others
Me and the others I mean like Walt Whitman, Will Rogers,
    Pushkin,
Sandburg, and the others and the others,
I feel like I ought to have a little word to say
Because I know you worry about it from time to time
Just why I can't ever be like any one or two of them
No matter if I pound my ears with the heaviest hammer in
    town
I just can't and I never could if I tried
And what is more on top of that I don't want to
Because I can't set here and look at my paper a half a day
    between each word
Like Walt Whitman could
And I can't talk without speaking like Pushkin was so good at
Nor I can't work for the bosses and against them like Rogers
    did
Nor I can't help from saying what come up in me to say
Like Sandburg was such a hand at
And like most of these other poem books I pick up to read
And lay down again in a hurry because they don't talk my
    lingo nor tongue

If I did think that Whitman did talk my lingo and thoughts
If I did think that Will spoke my dialect and feelings
If I even felt that Mr. Pushkin had said my plainest feelings
Or if Carl Sandburg had told my folkiest talk
Or if any truck driver or trip hammer man or diesel driver
   woman
Anywhere on this planet had said what I say
Well, then, I wouldn't even knock my fingernails off ten
   hours a day
Trying to cut out some old and newer thoughts and feelings
   to get said
I won't have much of a time speaking plain as Walt Whitman
I won't have too much of a wrastle thinking plain as Will
   Rogers
I won't have too much of a struggle with Carl Sandburg
Just because I'm not writing down their life nor case history
And just because they didn't write down my words and folk
   story
And because I saw and smelt a few foneylike words in Whit-
   man
Rogers, Sandburg, Pushkin, you and me, and everybody else
And this is the hard down reason why
I took off down this topsod row here to break out a new
   patch
For my own words and my own talk and my own feelings to
   sprout up in
This is why I like the others and hate the others and why
They like and hate and feel jealous and stiff-haired about me
   plowing in
In my odd and loose-jointed ways
And this is why I still argue and ask you, you reading me
   here,
To set yourself down with your pen or pencil in your hand
Or down on your seat or bench there in front of your type-
   writer

And write down for the whole race of us humans around here
The stuff and the things and the mistakes and the foney
  baloney
That me and these others used to win ourselfs a name with.
I got to quit now and go in the kitchen and smear another
  coat
Of tile glue around the mouth and rim of the water faucet
  where
We've got our garden hose screwed on and the water's been
  leaking.
And if this backyard here don't jump up lots greener lots
  faster
I couldn't look out at this window here and write no very
  good books
Of deathless prose and lifeless literature and fulkazongs and
  fulkaballits.

June 6, 1947

Prophet Singer

Somewhere way back in my mind, I can hear the boys in
the PX sing their old nickel beer songs tonight till the lonesome tears for home rose down out of their eyes. Their songs
are not war songs, not gunner songs, not shooting songs.

Their songs are back home songs, back on the old coffee
corner songs. Songs about brown eyes, blue eyes, black fireball eyes, eyes of all colors and every man around these old
beer tables sings with his head low and his eyes closed.

And he sees home while we sing.

I see my old self back home. I hear Marjorie and me rocking around singing to our kids. I hear the kids in their passion club next door to us, singing and grunting, hugging,

tickling, feeling and laughing into the lights of their youth club nickel fonograph.

I love to hear your houses sing. I love to hear your windows yell. I like the sounds of your chants that toss new grunts on the fire all night long.

I live really in a hope that when I do get out from this old pisky army camp that I'll hear every door and every window sing all night long till the new day cracks.

I ask you, Mister President, please let everybody everywhere sing all night long. Love songs, work songs, new hope songs. This will cure every soul in our jail, asylum, and sick in our hospital, too. Try it and see. I know. I'm a prophet singer.

June 1, 1948
Coney Island

Bound for Glory

After I wrote my book, *Bound for Glory,*
And you read through the pages of it,
You might have been one of the several
That wrote to me, or stopped me to ask me
When was I going to park my carcass down long enough
    again
To write you up another lifebound novel real and unreal
And so I'd just like to say here and now tonight
While we got this time and this place here to talk and to
    listen
That I've got a high feeling running in me

About a good book done well
I spend big hunks of my good money in bookstores progres-
sive
And I buy up every sort of a book from evolution to folk-
singery
From Charles Darwin to Leadbelly
From Pushkin through Sandburg on up to Woody Guthrie
And I still feel
That I just can't get printed the words I write into my novel
books
I think I've got a good ear and good eye for a good story
heard or seen
And I take in plenty of movies and most of the staged plays
around
And I've actually wrote up some of the longest and hottest
Pages and stacks of pages in the forms of novels and true
tales
But still there is something too slow and too plowy and
ploddy
For me to spend my time at fooling around with long novels
When I'd rather to hear a room full of my comrades and
friends
Sing out real loud on one of my songs
Which I've wrote, say, from the start to the finish
So before I turn out my lights here to call it a night
Let me just leave you with this plain in your head
That I've never heard nobody yet get a whole room full
Of friends and enemies both
To sing and to ring the plaster down singing out a novel
Like I've heard them sing out my songs already
And like I liked so much on the tips of my ears
I do aim to write out a couple or three booking tales I got
headed up
Sometimes in these first years about to come

Books I've already got started and several hundred pages
     torn up on
But outside of these two or three books
I'm going down the trail of folk songs and ballads old and
     new
And I aim to give us all some good true history songs to sing
With the highest gospel of religious fire on earth.

June 16, 1947
Coney Island on a hot crowded night in
June 1947, the first hot or crowded night this
season. Bugs are trying to knock their
brains out against my tube light so will see
you in the morning when the grass gets up.

Old Paper Sheets

These old paper sheets are my pile of money, I run my
thumb over them just like you do your bank notes there.

I'm my own bank and I'm my own boss,

I ain't never out of work,

My eye ain't never batting.

My hand feels always oily and my fingers always itchy,

Twenty-four hours every day I send mself out and around
to run hook lines.

I write what I see,

I write what I've seen,

[30]

I write things that I just hope to see

Somewhere farther along.

April 4, 1948
Newark, New Jersey
On the low end of
High Street

The Word I Want to Say

The word I want to say is easy to say, and yet is the hardest word I've tried to say.

It tries to make all of my feelings plain,

And what one word can I say that will say them all?

Most times I try to speak it, I never do get it said, and when I try to plan it, it always slips my plans and slips my tongue.

I am trying to be a singer singing without a dictionary, and a poet not bound down with shelves of books. My shelf of books is fairly high already, and many other words from out of other mouths are here and ready for me to lay with and to play with, but I try to skip those books all that I can and say my words with my two freer hands.

The word I want to say is here, and close, and free and easy on my lip and tongue, but seldom said, like some slick water fish that jumps through net holes fast as I can knot and loop. I know what my word means. I know what my word says. I know its weight and measure, its name, label, and trademark. I know its shape and feel, its house and home, I know its taste and smell, its body touch. I know my unsaid word better than my unsaid word knows me. The same as I know you better than you will ever know me.

This one word I want to say would make all clear between my wife and myself, or, rather, would make me as clear as my wife is. She is always the clearest of the two of us. I am always the foggy and the mixed-up one, and she is always the outspeaking, outthinking one. If I could just speak this one unsaid and unspoken word to her, things between us would be the limber and undanced dances they ought to be. Our house and our home is crippled and hurt just because of this one word I can't say nor speak.

This one word would make me know my children and would make my children know me. If I could just say this one word, my children's children would know that we are both just alike, that there is no difference in us big enough to separate and tear us apart. In our thoughts, I think, all of us could go around the world and know everybody on it if we could just find and speak this one same word.

It's not a secret word or a magic word. No word is secret. No word is magic. No word is hid. I've followed this one word now for several years, and around the house since I was born here. I've let it lead me by my finger out where the loose snow blows around these weedstems. I've climbed hand ladders of boxcars, shipsides, truck cabs, doors, fire escapes, wagons, and barn lofts. I've said it to cops, guards, vigilante men, soldiers and to sailors, to farm women and farm girls, to house women and to house girls, to hotel women and to hotel girls, to street women and to street girls, to men and boys shingling roofs in southern states, driving nails in western mountains, digging dirt in eastern places, painting and welding in every state in the Union. I've said this one word in every tongue and language and unto every color of face, lips, ear, and hair. To the brown, to the red, to the yellow, to the black skin and to the blackskin. You knew this word when you heard it spake, sung, motioned, signaled, or danced.

The odd thing is about this word that it is no one certain word, but fits in the ring and tone sound of every word. It is the word inside of all of our other words, the word that gives our words a shape and a form, and a clearer sense. This is the free word that no jail can hold, no cell can keep, no chain drag down, no rope can lynch, no weapon can hurt nor hinder. I say this word is that one word that makes all democracy clear, plain, and keeps democracy alive, the same as democracy keeps me alive, and I keep this one word alive. I will die as quick and as easy as I can to keep this one word living, because it keeps my whole race of people living, working, loving, and growing on to know more and to feel more. This is the word I want to say.

Names for Marjorie's and Woody's Kids' Parties

Hootenholler
Play Day
Kuttinup
Dance Around
Rigajig Party
Jump Up Party
Shootemup Afternoon
Whackemdown Time
Mow 'em Down Hour
Bloody Run Time
Kutie Pie Playtime
Hootenjump
Sugar Jump
Tootsie Whirl

Round I Go
See Me Grow
Groovey Shoe Time
Ribbon and Bell Party
Song and Ribbon Time
Quickstep High Time
Funtime

Joy Boys
Whirly Girls
Tippy Tap Toe Time
Slackyshoe Party
Lost Button Hootenyell
Pretty Funtime
Goofy Goodtime
Crazy Playtime
Lazy Hay Time
Woozie Juice Time
Song and Dance Time
Dance and Sing Time

Sweety Swing Time
Mighty High Time
Awful Good Time
Lotsa Funtime
Nuts and Jerk Time
Lose Your Shoe Time

Party Low Tide
Party High Tide
Song and Rough Time
What a Big Time
Time to Take Time
Time to Make Time
Time to Dance Time
Holey Shoe Time
Children's Wild Time
Old Folks Kiddin' Time
Family Big Time
Moon and Sun Time
Fire and Smoke Hour
Eat and Drink Time
Your and My Time

Child Sitting

Watching kids is the highest form of art in the world. It can be as bitter as a drink of carbolic acid or as sweet as a warm cup of new milk and wild honey.

The family doctor came to our house three days back and found me here on our bed moaning, groaning, with a splitting headache, a stiff back, a raw neck, a sore throat, a stuffed-up nose, and a crazy cough which I've had now for the past couple of weeks. He stuck his wooden paddle in my mouth, made me say Ah, and then touched my back and chest with his stainless steel listening tube which drew me up in worse pains than my two weeks of coughing. He rolled me over and over on the bed, made me cough again so he could listen to my gurgles. He wrote something down on a prescription paper, told me to use nose drops, and to stop smoking so

many cigarettes, not to drink any liquors, and to take a tea-
spoon of stuff every three hours. I sweated and had bad
dreams all night. I dreamed I saw the tobacco fighting the
nose drops, the cough medicine fighting my sore throat, the
aspirin fighting the soup in me, and I grunted each and every
time something struck a blow at something else. I remember
I grunted, like a man driving circus stakes with a sledge
hammer, whow, whow, whow, real slow, and real easy, but
Marjorie told me I kept her awake all night long. My sheets
were so wet they would have filled our bathtub if you'd have
wrung them out in it. But, well, I tried to die. I thought I did
die. I felt dead, and I was sort of glad to be dead. I was
better, though, next morning when Cathy sang a song in my
ear as she stood next to our bed. I felt well enough to take
her to school and she went piggy-back on my shoulders.

Cathy's teacher at the nursery school looked at Cathy's
tongue, nose, and ears, eyes, and said she looked okay, so I
waved goodbye to Cathy, and beat the sidewalks home
again. Marjorie ate her breakfast, cleaned the kitchen on her
hands and knees, and left to teach her classes of kids, grown-
ups, old folks, how to dance. She left at eleven-thirty.

I wrote on my deathless books, songs, stories, on my new
typewriter as fast as it would run for a few hours, then
things got all bogged down, and I took off in the late afternoon and went to see a gypo movie. I heard everybody in
the movie house coughing, spitting, hacking, rattling, and
whooping, and I said to myself, well, there's a world of us
that's got to lay off smokes, eats, drinks, and movies till we
get on our feet. I was a bit late going to Cathy's nursery
community center, but she was not so full of life and pepper
as she most times is. She walked along in her red ski suit and
didn't say much about the things going past. When we got
home, she sipped a sip of soup, and dabbed her face with
water, then went to bed.

Next morning she stayed in her bed and told Mommy that

her tummy ached. She drank some juice in her bed, then walked into our front room and climbed up onto our big double folding bed. Mommy called the doctor again. He asked some questions over the phone, Does her tummy hurt low down or high up, or over on the side? Are her eyes red like radishes and are her eyelids droopy and pink like? Is her nose stopped up? Throat hurt? Tongue coated with white and yellow stuff? And then he said, "Don't do anything until I get there." But Mommy had to go to work again before the doctor got there.

I was here with Cathy alone after he looked her over from stem to stern, and he told me to paint her throat with argyrol, to give her a tablespoon of milk of magnesia, and a half an aspirin tablet in a swallow of water every four hours. Cathy had a touch of fever and so she did not get out of bed while I tore out to the drugstore and back. I brought her a box of ten-cent crayons as a surprise and gave her a whole dime package of my three-hole typing paper.

Sam, the newspaper man, ran in with his arms full of coloring books, a jar of sticky paste, a big red balloon, another box of crayons, all sent from the candy store by Marjorie on her way to work. Sam ran back out again to sell his papers and magazines and Cathy was waving, " 'Bye, Sem." She held up the jar of paste first and told me, "Deddy, here, opinnit."

"Play with your other things," I told her. "Color all of those nice pictures in your color books, there. Cut out things with your scissors. Ahh, that's nice, nice, ah, and, ah, and dress all of your dolls up in their clothes, and draw me some good pictures on your paper there with your new crayons. Mommy will feel bad if she comes home and finds old sticky paste all over her sheets and blankets." I was pacing all up and down the floor all around the bed like a bumble bee lost from his hive. "That's it. That's a good girl. Old Santy'll fill your stockings and shoes besides with all kinds of nice things. That's it. Here. I'll put the paste away on a shelf in your room. Here."

"But, Deddy, I wanta just paste."

"Color."

"Paste."

"Cut."

"Paste, Deddy. Silly. Don't ya know what paste is?"

"Draw me a nice big, big, big picture."

"I'll paste ya one."

"Dolls."

"My dolls ask me ta paste 'em a s'prize."

"Draw with a pencil."

"But, Deddy, ya cain't paste nuthin' with a pencil."

I sat down at my typewriter here at the head of our bed, rolled in some pages of a ship story I'm writing about my days in the merchant marines, the two torpedoes I got out of three invasions, the people I met, bombed cities I walked through, the ships and planes fighting, the V-bombs I've seen, and paid no more mind to her until sometime later. She took the phone off the table when it rang and said, "Howllo. Who? Laundry? Nooo. This is me. Cathy. Cathy. Who are you? Cathy's my name. Stackabones. My mommy's name is Marjorie. I'm not any laundry. What's your name? Wrong what? Wrong number? That's a funny name. He hunged up, Deddy."

"Now, you hang up." I kept on writing.

"But, Deddy, I cain't."

"Huhm. Why not?"

"It's stuck to my hand. Lookatit. Deddy, git me loose."

"Lord have mercy on us sinners. Cathy. Stacky Wacky. Jackie Whacker. Cracker Jacker. Rackety Stackity. Look at you. Look at me. Look at that telephone. Look. Look. Look at Mommy's and Daddy's bed. Just take yourself a look at that bed."

"Unstick me."

"Didn't I tell you in plain words, Cathy, not to open up that bottle of paste on your Mommy's and Daddy's bed?"

"Unstick my hand from th' phone. I hafta paste more."

"More? More paste? Well, I've done all I can do. It's no fault of my own. It's her fault, it's your mama's fault, for ever leaving me alone here in this house with you, anyhow. I've got work to be done. I can't drop everything I'm working on and just spend my days keeping you from tearing the house down. Go ahead. Here's the washrag, warshcloth, whatever the devil you call it. Here. Warsh your own paste off of your own hands. I don't care what you do from now on. My work is just as important to me as your mama's work is to her. All right, so she teaches a few people how to flip their heads around in the air and how to dance."

"I danc'd in her big school oncet, didn't I, Deddy? 'Member? You put on my overalls and I carried my dress down in my shopping bag. 'Member? Don'tcha? Don'tcha 'member, Deddy?"

"I wisht you was with her today."

"But the doctor let me look down his mouth with his flashlight an' he said I hadda sore neck an' I said he was fulla mish an' mishmush, an' he said I couldn't say Ahhhhh, 'cause he had a stick stuck down my froat, an' Mommy told me Santy Clawss wood come see me if I stayed home nice an' let Deddy paint my tonsels with that ol' brown stuff, an' I hafta make a paper chain for my doctah, an' for my Mommy an' a cut-out pumpkin with crosseyes past'd for my Deddy, an' I hafta lay my heady down in Mommy's bed 'cause my bed's too little to hold alla my papers an' toys an' past'd things. An', Deddy, it's time for you to cook my soup, but don't cook me any soup, 'cause I'm too sick and I don't want any soup. You can make you some soup, but don't make me any soup, 'cause I don't feel like I like soup. An' I don't like crackers, either. I hafta paste a pumpkin that's gay on Halloween Day on Chris'mus card white on Thanksgivin' Night."

The whole box of Kleenex tissues were pulled out and pasted on top of one another, like diapers folded flat in a laundry. The color books had paste between their pages. She had cut out chains, pumpkins, baskets, fruit of every kind, masks with eyes, noses, mouths, that looked like people you know. She had smeared her cheeks with paste like Mommy does her cold cream, and painted her fingernails with it, the way her grandma showed her. Everything on the bed was stuck to everything else. I picked up the pasted basket to carry away into Cathy's room and the rest of the mess on the bed all followed me. There was no more paste in the jar, so she asked me for a new package of my typing paper and drew several dozen pictures with her Crayolas. Each page, she made me stop what I was doing and write down with pen and ink what the picture was all about.

One was, "All About Peter and the Worf an' here's Grand-papa with th' trees all around him." Another one was, "A Zoo with every kind of an Animal you are looking for." Another was, "A Ferry Boat with a Pumpkin Driver on Top." One was, "A Big House with Every Color of People in It." "An Apple, a Pear, a Peach, an' My Mommy Dancing." One said, "This Is the Alligator Biting the Mother Turtle an' th' Mother Turtle Bites the Alligator on His Tail." Another one, "Here is My Spider Chasing after My Bunny Rabbit and My Bunny Rabbit Hasta Run Real Fast." This took up most of my whole afternoon. Everytime I wrote down the next words, she drew another picture and yelled out some more to be written down. She drew one that was called, "What th' Hell Ya Think This Is?" And one that was called, "You Don't Know What in the Devil You're Talkin' About." She even drew three separate pictures, each one titled, "A Big Car Getting Rained On All Over." I don't know why I wrote her words down on all of these drawings. It's just a little thing I started doing a year or so ago and now it's a wild thing, a thing of no control, spreading fire, a blaze, a smoke, some kind of a thing like the black market, like gambling, like using dope, it's something that has got so big that I can't stop it by myself. When these days come on which I am left entirely alone in the house with Cathy, Miss Stackabones, I'm whipped, I'm outwitted, out run, out classed, and out maneuvered. My mind leaves off where hers begins. My ideas stop where hers start in. My brain is no match for her with her sly and slick ways of making me do everything she wants me to.

She sang songs while she drew her pictures after her paste was all gone, and forced me to take down the words as she sang them. I've got several hundred of her songs already written down. I've sold two albums of phonograph records of kids' songs just by putting little tunes and guitar notes to her songs she sings. I've written stories of a dozen kinds and mailed them away to the papers and the magazines. I've planned a twelve months' concert tour of the dances of Cathy's to be done by Marjorie (our mama), with two hours of Cathy's songs (by me), and still I've not scratched the first crust of top dirt in her garden of the soul.

This is her second day of being at home inside with her cold, and she's up and around, and lots better. She is dressed in all of our clothes of this and other years, she has had me tying bow knots all morning long, she has smeared herself all over with lipstick and rouge, stripped her skin naked and danced about the place like a windward spirit. The house looks like the big bed did yesterday, only, the bed still looks like it did. I've written down a dozen songs today, and taken down the names of a dozen more pictures. There's not enough recording companies in the world to make records of all she makes up. Not enough radios or movie studios to catch one tenth of what she floats through every day. Her

dance around
and around
and aroun

woody Guthrie
1951

songs are rated by *Newsweek,* by *Time,* by the *Daily Worker,* as the top-notch best in the children's album field and, yet, here I am, a lost man, a sick man, a man that needs help, advice, and good words. She's in her room now singing through the wall:

> I gambled to lose In Newport News
> And I drunk in Baltimore
> I took some trips on some foamy ships
> An' I'm aimin' ta sail some more, some more,
>
> Aimin' ta sail some more.

Dead Fathers

Rosylee didn't show up today in gym class.

Her daddy died. Some of the kids in the class didn't send her no flowers, no telegram, no letter.

That's why Rosylee wasn't here in gym class today.

Some just didn't even know about her father dying.

Some knew but just didn't know how to tell her.

Some wondered what good their few little words could do.

Some choked up in the neck when they thought about him.

Some didn't have enough money to write or to send a wire.

Some had seen their own fathers die and pass away without any too many stacks or piles of letters and telegrams with flowers.

Others have seen other fathers, sons, mothers, sisters, brothers, uncles, and all, fall somewhere under the dust of a bullet or the smoke of a bomb.

Rosylee lives in a great big out-of-doors country hill estate with whole hills and valleys of leaves and trees around her to help her to get over the losing of her daddy. Most of us haven't even got this, Rosylee.

I am a daddy. I am a father. Six have come my way to slap me on my back and ask for a cream cone..

But, when I do go down, whichever trail I do go out on, no matter how it comes about or happens, Rosy, I don't want good pals to have any such silly falling-outs about cards, letters, wires, nor money, nor houses, nor flower buds. None of these count. My kids will love their friend that can't or don't write, and they'll love their friend that does try to send something.

If any of my relatives or friends sends up any such a silly squabble about me after I get gone, I swear that I'll turn off into a howling lightning storm and break every window out of every house you move into.

Rosy. Rosy Lee. Go back to that gym class and cry your head off and wipe your tears down all over your gymminy suit till the colors are all smeared all over you and the rest of them. Just tell everybody you stumped your big toe and fell down for a little bit, but you're back up again and all right now.

June 7, 1948

My Best Songs

My best songs will be the ones that never rhyme;
They will be my songs about the bare limbs and the blos-
soms;
And I'll always walk and talk and ask myself,
How can the limb that is bare set itself up to judge
The trunks and the limbs, twigs, and sprigs that are in blos-
som?

And I would fight and die my best,

I believe, to fight on the seed that is sprouting, growing,
blooming,

And fight against the things, plant, animal, human, that try
to tell my spirit of life to stop its blossoming, blooming,
and its seeding and its planting.

I love men and women that are plain and honest about their
own feelings, because, how can your feelings rule and
judge other lives if you're not able to make your own
highest and deepest feeling plain in several ways?

I see worlds and worlds of rooms and desks
where men and women are gathered around in robes,
coats, suits and dresses, to say what I shall write, speak,
talk, and sing.

And they tell me that I am locked and barred from singing
the true feelings of my nakedest skin.

Why can't you sing songs nor act lines about your naked skin,
when I see my nakedest skin as a thing thousands of times
prettier than the greatest and grandest scene of landscape,
hill, mountain, river, sand dunes, sand ripples, and wild
trees in open canyons. Why can't I sing the most beautiful
song of them all, the doings and feelings of my unclothed
and unhid self?

You are gathered here this morning to burn my finest papers,
You are here in this room at this very hour to tell me that
there is something ugly, vile, vulgar about me, somewhere,
somehow, someway. I excuse your ignorance. I can think
of only one way to fight you back, and the whole race of
man is fighting you back in this same way, by just standing
to the one side and laughing at your sad condition of
paralysis and death. [one of the wonderful things to remember
here is that V.G. is lying paralysed in a hospital bed]
I am not ashamed of me nor ashamed of myself.

I am not ashamed of me in any of my positions nor moods

[47]

nor attitudes. I will fight your ugliness with my very health and beauty. I must try my level best to display my beauty, to sing and dance in my feelings, the pretty feelings, to overcome, override, and to overflow your bogholes and wallows of neurotic fear, hate, greed. You are spreading a worser gospel of hate than just simple race hate, you are spreading the gospel and the sermon that I'd ought to hate and to fear and to weep and to mourn about my only good possession, my own self.

You tell me that I am something so sorry and terrible that I'd ought to feel my worst pain and misery when I drop my robes and rags to one side and show you the only pretty sight in this world. You say I am wrong to lay flat on my back and to kick my legs uncurtained around in your sacred air.

You are a worser thief than the worst and the bloodiest robber, pirate, bandit, or second-story operator, because you are robbing me of my own human pride and dignity, of my own happiness to dwell here in my own flesh. You smear your hot tar and your feathers of imbecilic and spasmodic, epileptic fears onto my most private and most glorious grounds. You set off these charges and demolitions in my fairest orchard, you dynamite my dreamiest gardens, and you blow up my most classic park, my most classic gallery, observatory, and my finest museum. You spray acids and wrecking chemicals all up and down my most perfect workshop and laboratory. I, my own naked and nakedest self, I am warmer, fairer, more beauteous than all of your houses and homes and your rattling towns and railroaded cities, and just because you feel all of these narrow, hateful, mean, downhearted, downcast, and downtrodden feelings about your own physical bodyself is no reason why you have the right to pass a law of our land making me a criminal for feeling happy, healthy and freely pretty inside of my own body and self. You have no right to burn my books that tell you how I feel about my skin and bones and hot flesh. You can't burn my films, my scripts, my papers and my handbills. These all belong to you and if you burn them a million times in a billion piles, and if the flames and the sour smokes rise up as high as the outer planets, still, still, you've not burned up one little stray and solitary thought that rolls on through my body's universes.

Give me a world a thousand times
Where somebody somewhere on it is not blind or dead. Give me the vision of my world with the true thinking true believers singing and dancing and sweating on it, rubbing bellies of creation and stuck together with the glues, foams, juices or running and wheeling love. Give me a planet where the dead leaves do not dictate it nor rule it like death.

Call up the vision gardens and order me a newer planet to live and to work on. This old earth is too bilboed and shackled, too chained, too sacked and sandbagged, too beat, too narrow, too filthy, too vile and poisonous, and too near death for me to dwell or to grow on.

Oh, you can throw your dust grains at me and I won't care too much, and you can sail your atom balls at me and I won't shiver too hard, because I've practiced running and ducking and dodging so much that I'm a pretty fair hand at ducking chemical units. Blast away at me, if you want to, if it makes you feel any finer, fire away at me with one of your blistering gasses, or one of your bottled diseases, a tube or two of your plagues and smothering bombs, and maybe I can find some way to run somewhere and hide most of my body away from the impacts and concussions of your bombings. But, please, please, don't strike at me with this hypnotic and self-fearing belief and religion, this religion that preaches at me to hate and to fear, to feel sad and ashamed for my own human naked flesh skin and body.

This is the one destruction that I can't live over. This is the one germ which I can't duck nor dodge. This is the one chemical, the one acidic mixture that I can't untie nor cut my way out of. This is the one electric chair that I can't wiggle loose from and run. This shameful feeling of my own self, this fearful nervousness in my own soul and body, this would make me feel so bitter and so hateful inside of my own body that I would hate and fear every other human body on the face of this earth. This whole thing that you mark out as just a "purple passage" in words of my soul, this is really the one color that I've always loved and admired to feel, taste, and to see. Purple is not my only color nor my pet color, but purple does wonderful good to my soul while my eyes are dancing around through its purples. And all of a sudden, all in a flash, all in a snap of your fingers, you are telling me that all of my purple shadow, corners, pages, and hues, all of my purples in any shading, grading, mixture or form, must be erased and rubbed out from the scenes of my whole life. Goodbye to my purple. No, I say, Hello there, purple, and Goodbye to any living or dead soul that does not dance and sing in the breeding blossoms on my purples.

My body is naked now, and it was born naked.

No matter how I dress up or undress, I am naked. By the cracks and creaks of the morning's breakings, I am naked. The hours of early morning find me naked and I find the hours and the morning just as naked as they find me. The hours when I eat my meals are terrible hours of nakedness. Every bite I eat rubs my naked lips against the naked skin of my food. My naked hand holds its naked glass to

my naked tongue and I drink my naked drink down over
my naked teeth and throat and down into my naked
stomach. And I am really the least naked person in New
York City, Coney Island, or any other naked place. I see
myself always naked and I see your form and shape always
naked. I see you standing there in front of me talking to
me about our work, your work, my works, or somebody
else's works, and no matter how many rags or pretty duds

you pile over yourself, I see you stripped naked when you walk past me. All of us are naked. All of us come here naked and we go from here naked. Overalls, dresses, work pants, dress pants, coats of fur, coats of cloth, jackets of water and windproof goods, gloves, hats, socks and stockings, shoes of every color, none of these, not any of these hide your nakedness from me, nor my nakedness from you. Your naked thoughts I always know, and my naked notions and cravings you always see as naked.

I love the very sound of the naked word. I love the very picture and vision of you that I call naked because I see you as naked. The best and juiciest of humanly truths are our naked truths. Our finest honesty is our naked honesty. Our greatest feelings are those ideas and inventions which we touch in their most naked places. You are not ashamed of any of your naked places. It is always your places that are not clothed which make you feel your best, your gayest, gladdest, and your happiest, healthiest. I feel the same way as you feel about my naked places. None of my places feel their real best till I get them uncovered, unhid, and stripped down naked. I love no woman nor man my very tip and top till I see you or help you to get naked. I don't even pretend to know you my best nor your best till I have known you bare and clean and naked. I love my own naked thoughts and naked feelings more than I ever could love my draped and covered moods and hopes. My naked plans are my only really living plans. My naked blueprints are the only prints I can see by well enough to raise up my newer world out of this pile of wreck and wreckage. I work with naked hands and speak my naked words. I love most to undress words and thoughts which you have buried and hid from my eye.

Maybe you don't want to live the naked way that I live. The way that you want to live is okay by me. I'm not here to say that you ought to hang by your thumbs nor your toes just because you wish to drape, to undrape, to change draperies any time you wish to. But, I'm afraid to say that I want to dwell in these old curtains and laces of old worn-out customs and superstitions, older rules and mossy laws. Maybe you feel your best when you live in your world where your garments are picked and chosen by some room or table rounded with censors and with judges. You may feel snug and secure in the kind of rugs and robes that they pick out for your thoughts to wear. Maybe you feel good and glad that these judges are doing all of this deciding for you and for your children, but they'll not ever live to see the sky of the day nor the night that I will let them judge my own nakedness for me and for my children. I work hard every day to dig my own children out from under the old piles of sexual and physical confusions that the noble judgers have heaped on my kids. I don't want any more of this mental acid sprinkled nor sprayed with quiet whispers on the brain cells of myself nor of my children. But, maybe you enjoy letting these people around this censored table do your picking and your choosing and your living, working, loving, going, coming, and eating and drinking, your reading and your thinking for you. But bury me beneath the willow on that day when I let such a roomful of judges try to do a universe full of thinking and dreaming and planning and working for me.

In my most naked thoughts, I've always laid flat on my back on the beds of living leaves and grass, and counted the tree buds with my hands and the night stars with my toes. I, as a man, could not pose like I feel like a man, nor one half of a man, if I was ashamed of the hairs on my head. And, if you've seen me, you know that my head of hair is well known to many faces and hands. My hair grows like the underroots of stems and stalks, and my doctor book tells me that I can always judge the health of a person by the hair of his or her head. I am prouder of my head of hair than of any song, poem, ballad, book, play, or which what, that I'll ever turn out. I am prouder of the hairs on my body than I am of my artistic works. And I feel really prouder of the hairs around my male organ, hairs around my balls and my sack, hairs up and down my legs, hairs in between my legs, hairs that grow all over me, hairs all over me, I am prouder about my hairs than about any of my other worldly goods. And the men and women and the kids that I call the best ones are the ones that make jokes, sing, and tell long madeup stories and tales about the naked hairs and feelings between their legs.

Your positions of breeding could never be any too decorated nor dressed to suit my feelings.

Your feathers of attracting and your shirts and skirts of calling could never be piled on too thick nor too thin to suit me fine.

Your hats of every hue and tone, your pants and panties of every color, your shoes of every fancy sort, you couldn't pull a garter onto your leg that I would ban, censor, nor blame. Your work gloves of canvas and leather never would cause me to haul up before my judging bar, neither would I call you up before my eye to make fun of you for pulling your fingers into the finely spun gloves you use in your trips of hunting and finding.

I know that the most fun you get out of your life is your dressing up and your undressing. I say that dressing and undressing, draping and undraping, is a form of art and science as high and as noble, higher and nobler, than any I've seen. Where is there a judge with such a warm light glinting in his or her eyes as I see in my own eyes, and in your own eyes? I never will swap this warm light you see in my eyes for any colder lights you see in these eyes of our censors.

You seem to know about humans what our best scientists know about dogs, hogs, horses, cattle, chickens, sheep, fishes, monkeys, birds, and gorillas, that my highest and greatest feeling comes to me when I see the best uses made of feathers, drapes, colors, decorations, and costumes. I say the best use is to make the breed better, the brood better, the mating and the nesting, and the whole species and kind better an ounce or a drop or maybe a great deal.

Go ahead, use ribbon and your lace to pull me towards you, and I'll use every trick of shadow and shading to pull you closer to me. And, as for the pull and the pulling, well, the closer, the warmer, the nicer and the better. Be just the opposite of ashamed about your decks and rigs and costumings. Be glad. Be upstanding and be proud. Your face is already lifted towards the sky and its lights make me wild and crazy for the touch and taste of you.

Your hips can't make a motion which I can say I hate. Your muscles can't make a move that I will try to erase out. Your blood can't run in a way which I will stop and send back. Your legs can't open in a way that I will arrest and give a summons. Your thighs can't move in a way I'll look up behind my bars. And those rumps, hips, and belly muscles of yours, you could never shimmy nor shake them in a way which I would drag off to my chain gang. Your back, your ribs, your breasts never could cause me to latch you away in my psycho cellar. I love most and my very most to see you wiggle your patch of hairs in every kind of a design, pattern, crisscross, roll, sway, and twitch. I see and taste no sweat any more honest than those drops you have in joy there between your legs. Your face looks its holiest, its proudest, its finest and gladdest this minute as you do roll here like I roll. This look and smile, or this half-smile, across your face right this very minute, your hair shaking above your eyes, makes Woody Guthrie feel like a lost man getting found.

You move here in front of me and around me and make me see why it is our loster folks that feel their lostness and want, not only to stay in their lost places, but to drag all of us found ones in there with them. It is those who have thrown away their cake that ache and burn to see us scatter our crumbs and icings. It is they that say that such words and such thoughts as I am now writing will never occupy space on the printed and bounded pages. Why? Who? The ones that traded their hip dances for a sack of insane fearful notions. Those who shut their mind and their eye to the lights you throw out around you from your heat and your passion. Those that are afraid of some object or another somewhere in between the human legs. Those that got afraid to touch the knob on the door of creation when it was within the very touch of their finger. Those afraid to taste the living lights of being alive as a human being on this earth planet. Those that were too busy snatching and grabbing at smaller toys to smell these unsmelled odors along creation's trailways. Those ashamed somehow for creation its whole self.

And, if creation itself can't satisfy your eyes nor your lips,
How on earth can I do anything that will satisfy creation and the censor at the same time?

I live in my very blood as a creator
And to create is my only work.
And when I am not creating today more than I created
yesterday
or last night, these are the days that I go wild and crazy

and do all sorts of wilder crimes that I never would do if I had found my way to reach out and shake hands with creation.

And sex is creation.

Sex is the secret key and the higher way to creation, until sex is gassed and shot full of fears. When sex turns to fear, then every drop of clear waters in the universe turns green, stagnates, and goes sour to the taste and sickly to my touch. In whose eyes does sex burn its clearest, the black-robed adjudger or the jitterbugs sweating through their shirts and dresses? I could, but I'll not, force my hand to write a letter of a hundred pages to frighten and scare you about your native and natural sexual movements. No, it would be better that my hands were chopped off at my elbows and my tongue padded with dry corn shucks. For me to stand up and to elect myself as the judge and the jury of what moves and motions and what decorations my own sex of my own race will and will not take? If I stood up and waved my hands and fists around in this room and let my lips drip ropes and foams of poison words about your sex feelings, I would be lots worse of a dictator than Hitler ever got to be, and I'd spread more wrecked towns and bodies than all of our wars and guns have wrecked. I could tell the winds which ways to blow, tell the sun which ways to shine, tell the twigs which ways to bend, tell the trees which ways to lean and to leaf out, tell the rivers which ways to run, tell the hills which ways to hump and the prairies which ways to rise and fall, but not one little word could I take enough dope nor drink enough bottles to curse out against your native motions of breeding.

So, I say, go ahead on, and on, and toss your hair around in your air there, as this is the sort of tossing that makes your hair roots strong and your hair stems sparkley. Twist your shoulders around me here and do funny things in the sun with your arms and your hands. Swing your breasts and lift them up your proudest to my eye, and roll your stomach and bowels here where I can glimpse you. And keep it up. Take big breaths of air and let me see your lungs rise and fall with your breasts. Just come close enough to me once in a while to brush your hair and your skin against my lips, this is all of the judging I will do to you.

Throw your hips to the side. Throw first your first hip, second your second hip. And roll your first hip my way, then roll your other hip in a drop, in a sway, out, down and away, and then back up to me again, and then do our dance all around and about our spot here. For what other reasons are hips manufactured? To hide away? To shackle down? To lace up like a lunatic jacket? To ball and to chain down and to wear blisters of hard and slow work only? No, but if our hips are going to be healthy ones and lift lots of serious loads, then we've got a hundred more good reasons why we ought to roll them at each other, and to dance them in front of our eyes, and to jump, to leap, to wiggle, shimmy, to melt and to run full of the juices we'll drink to our glory. Jerk, balance, lift, and fall. And, let this be ribboned and tagged as your finest gift to me and my only gift to you.

If there is a prettier sight than you dancing here around me, I've never seen that sight. If somewhere down my road of living there is going to be a sight fairer to me to see and to smell and to taste, I can't even begin to dream of what that sight might be, and I don't care to crave for it right at this minute. Let the oncoming things take care of those coming on. Let these best things right this minute not be crowded nor pushed nor smeared around with a herd of thoughts of our past nor even a batch of our thoughts about the things the future is bringing. Dance in your highest bubbles right here for me this minute. Lift and stretch your muscles, sinews, tissues, and skin here now your wildest and your nakedness for my eyes to grow on and for my soul to grow on. Those who have seen this forest patch of viney hairs tangled and curled like corkscrews of honey silk, those that know of this sight as plain as I see it in the moves you make, those that see your hips move, belly roll, and your lips shine out, those will surely not stand up to say that such an earthly sight is never supposed to be seen inside the published covers of any books. Those who have felt your heat of your skin and those who have spent days kissing your hairs will write my name down in coming history books just for jotting down this dim faint dream about you here on my dreaming sheets.

I'm not ashamed of the state I come from, Oklahoma, and Oklahoma's real soul is not ashamed to have me come from her sandy hills and stickery weeds. I'm not ashamed of the belly of the mother and the father that I sprung from, and they're not ashamed of me at the bottom of their hearts. I'm not one ounce ashamed of the natural fact that I did drop down and did squeeze my way out from my mama's womb and from amidst those hairs she grew between her legs. Not being ashamed of this, I have never been sourly ashamed of any thought, passion, feeling, nor mood that comes and goes through me. I've been frozen stiff a few times along the sides of roads, been chased by the clubs and guns of sheriff and deputy, been on top of fast freights in lightning storms and thunderstorms, been in cyclones and floods, been through a dozen deadly droughts and dust storms, and been through every kind of a fear and discouragement there is, and been through the mills of marriage more times than just one. I've been bankrupted a thousand times and wasted lots of time and money, but I never did feel guilty about any of this because I was torpedoed two times in the merchant marines during the war and I figure that whatever guilty feelings I owed to the race I paid off by these two torpedoes, and I paid off some more by laying out eight months in the army with a uniform on. So, my woman came to me so strong and so plain while I was at sea and in the camps that I swore and vowed that I was going to have to find love at its fullest and highest in order to make up for the wet dreams in my ship and army bunk. Every other man felt this same way. Several hundred thousand that I spoke to felt this same way. I went about with naked visions of naked, naked, naked you in front of my eyes for so many months that I vowed and swore that I would eat you up from your head down to your toes if you would so freely allow me to do it. I smelled your skin and your hairs just as plain, plainer, those days and nights on those troopships and in those army cots. I made you such a thing of glory in my mind that I wanted to lick you down like a big pile of dark brown sugar.

If there is a prettier sight on earth than those patched hairs between your legs, I've never seen nor heard about it. If there's a prettier sight than this long and viney root that stands up here between my legs, I've certainly never seen that. My pecker hard, my pecker soft and limber, my balls, my sack and my bag, my crotch, my legs, my root, my rod, this climbing long and jumping pole, this thing that is my gate of life, this door of mine through which we flow, this cord, this rope, this prong that I pass my finest creation through, I pass my own self through, I pass you down and out and in and through, this planting tool, this hose, this dong, dick, this stick and rod and staff of birth.

These visions come to me at my present age of thirty-four.

It is very true that, at some later age, I might feel that for my own self, that, well, that this sort of stimulation and exercise is not needed any more. My glands, my testicles, my breast bones and thigh bones might operate to mix up different feelings in me at some other age. I am singing here for us thirty-four yearlings. But when I am sixty-four I'm sure that I'll not ask all of you thirty-four yearsters to act like us sixty-fours act. I give unto each year of you this mental and physical right and duty to move your moves and to sing your songs that fit you the nicest.

I see headlines every day in the papers how some fair and pretty girl got raped, robbed, slugged and killed by some man or boy that had his natural sex feelings twisted around into such a terrible thick tangle of senseless junk that he thought sex was a city or a town that he had to march out and capture. He felt like it was some kind of battle that he had to fight, some fort, some trench, some hill or valley or mountain he had to fight to win. He met up with some girl that was partly filled with old fears about the naked self and sex, she could not understand his real sex feelings and he could not make them plain on account of his own older fears in his own self. What looked so beautiful whirled and changed into a windstorm and a rainstorm of the most miserable kind on earth. He left her because he could not find satisfaction there, she could not find it in him, and the lick knocked the two of them off into a fit of blind staggers in which nothing made any real sober sense. He felt like sex had been the death of him, she felt like sex had been the death of her, and both of them made up their minds to be the death of sex. Death got into his mind and into her mind. She spread her death in the form of deadly diseases. And when his feelings of sex got strong in him again he hid in the dark to beat and to kill the prettiest girl he laid eyes on, and maybe he killed two or three other girls which the papers failed to mention. Or there were seven such killings which the papers did not print. All charged up to your fears and shames that you have added onto the male root and spread inside of the female womb.

So, I ask you and tell you, kick your legs around in the air for me, and keep your womb clean for me. Spread your legs apart now and let me put this several inches of new life and lights into your plowed grounds, inside your hole and your nest, inside where you can bathe and warm it in all of your slick oils and salves. Let me come slow enough so as not to do you misery. Let me come in as slow as you want me. Let me hold you as you spread your knees nice and wide for me to lay my heavy load down here on your stomach. I will be so light and so easy that you will not even know that I am here in you. Your good feelings will make you forget all about me, my name, my color, my age, my politics, my religion, or any of these same things of your own. Hunch your hips and your hairs against my belly and against my hairs. And I will stay here in you and through you and all here about you till your eyes have closed to the sights of both of us and see only yonder prettier lights which light up the plains and hills in the lands of creation. And let me be man enough to stay here in you till your whole spirit is satisfied and your soul comes down to rest again here where I'm holding you. My pecker will still be in you. You can roll your second fit and spell and my shaft will go on and on deeper and deeper in you. This is what you will like about me. I will rub it against you every move you make day and night, and will always hold it against you so that you can feel its size, its shape, its heat and how hard it is. I will rub your hips, your legs with it, your knees and your stomach with it, and your back and breasts, your neck and your ears and lips with it. I will ease it so slow and easy into you that you will just go right on with your dreaming and your rolling. I will squirt such sprays of my seeds up against your organs that you will beg me and bite me and nibble me and kiss me and beg me again to squirt more into you and to shoot them harder. My seeds will drip down around your walls and ooze out from around my rod between your rumps. I am this kind of man and I love you in this kind of a way, a way that makes me want to see you dance naked all around me and to push your belly up against my nose so that I can kiss and lick your hairs down slick with our foams and honeys. And this over and over. And this on and on and on.

February 6, 1947

Good Married Daughter

To you, good daughter, you just now got your man and got married, you found the other 99% of your love dreams.

I can't tell you goodbye, because your love for your man is mostly a big loud hello.

All I can tell you about your man, girl, is this, if you give him 999/1000ths of the curious loves that he feels and burns and craves for,

and,

If you hold back some one little 1/1000ths part of loves rolls and tumblings, then like one little bullet,

Your holdback

Will knock him down hurt and staggering like a swatted fly.

O' smarty, snooty, genius of a daughter, go heal your man like the fly heals the crippled fly—with those slick juices of your lips and tongue—

Give your man his bath or he goes dead—

[63]

So, hello, my freshly married daughter, hello to the secret of all earth's healings.

The miracle of love—the love that heals.

October 21, 1948

Way Over Yonder in the Minor Key

Chorus:

> Ain't nobody that can sing like me
>> Way over yonder in the minor key
>> Way over yonder in the minor key
>
> Ain't nobody that can sing like me.
>> I lived in a place called Okfuskee
>> I had a little girl in a holler tree
>> I said, Little Girl, it's plain to see
>> Ain't nobody that can sing like me.

Chorus

>> She said it's hard for me to see
>> How one little boy got so uglee
>> Yes, my Little Girly, that might be,
>> But there ain't nobody that can sing like me.

Chorus

>> We walked down by the Buckeye Creek
>> To see the Frog eat the Goggle-Eyed Bee
>> To hear that west wind whistle to the east
>> There ain't nobody that can sing like me.

Chorus

>> Oh my little Girly will you let me see
>> Way over yonder where the wind blows free
>> Nobody can see in our holler tree
>> And there ain't nobody that can sing like me

Chorus

> Her mama cut a switch from a cherry tree
> And laid it onto she and me
> It stung lots worse than a hive of bees
> But there ain't nobody that can sing like me.

Chorus

> Now I have walked a long long ways
> I still look back to my tanglewood days
> I've led lots of girls since then to stray
> Saying, ain't nobody that can sing like me.

Chorus

The first two verses of this song come to me on the ninth of September while I was doing KP out in Scott Field, Illinois. I hummed it over to myself for a couple of months, or seven, and then took a notion today that I would finish it up. This song made up by Woody Guthrie, 3520 Mermaid Avenue, Brooklyn 24, N.Y., March the fifth, wife in town working, daughter in nursery school, jug dry, temperature warmer. A March wind is marching down along the ocean looking at the wreckage that washed in last night.

Atty. Gen'l. Tom Clark

BROOKLYN, NEW YORK
JANUARY 12, 1949

ATTY. GEN'L. TOM CLARK

DEAR SIR:

Radio station WNYC today is talking about the disease called cancer. Cancer is a disease that is partly caused by fear and kept aliving by other kinds of fears. It spreads in the

tissues of nervous fear; it travels in the celltowns of fears that rot out the nerves and highlines.

It can be started by fear. Planted with fear. Plowed and raised and seeded in the skylights of fear. The kinds of fear which keep cancer living and spreading, can and do keep other such diseases living and going. Like tuberculosis, venereal diseases, nervous diseases, heart diseases, bone diseases, ear eye nose and throat diseases; and I am asking you this morning to ask your own soul and conscience, sir, have you done anything to squirt any more poison of fear into the public bloodveins?

Have you caused anybody else to worry, to wonder, to be tricked, fooled, blinded, by the troubling fear that lives in the terrible jungle of worrying about your job? Worrying about low wages, worrying about high prices, fear about not being able to get into some kind of a better house and home?

Did you cause any living human anywhere on the face of the earth to take on any more bothersome, tiresome, terrible fears?

Fears about the war? Useless fears about another war on its bloody way to our streets and fields? Fears about the wild crazy use of our atom bomb? Fears about not being able to do the kind of work which every free person craves to do? Fears about not being able to make love, to get married, to breed and raise up a family, to house, to shelter, and to feed and clothe your family? Fears of losing everything you've been building up all of your life? Fears about taking down sick with no money to pay for medicine nor nurse nor doctor nor hospital? Fears about gambling and losing? Fears about empty stores, no customers and locked doors? Fears about no shipping, fears about no trading, fears about no freighting, no moving, no trucking, no loading, no jobs on the decks of our tied up rusty bottom boats and ships which stand still now because our big shots will not ship nor sell things to whole nations of people that think along some line of body politics which you hate and fear?

[67]

What about the fears of the rise in the crime figures? Kids in their teens on the skids to the jails? Kids in their prime knocked out like broken lamps on account of not being able to find a chance to work, to be useful, to get paid, to have the joys of working, spending, shopping, and buying along the display windows? The use of splints, frames, and plaster casts cannot even touch within ten thousand miles, sir, of the real cause nor the real sure cure for the terrible lack of teachers, doctors, nurses, scientists, interns, students, in the fields of the healing arts and sciences.

There is only one cure for all of this, and that cure has already been found in millions of windows and streets around the world. That cure is socialized healing. Socialized medicine. Socialized living, socialized working, socialized thinking, and socialized resting, sleeping, seeding, breeding, which you may or may not be fearful about.

If you are full of fears about socialism, sir, then you are surely spreading your killing fears through your own self and through the whole civilized worlds; if you are trying to hold back this only certain cure for all of our hands and our brains (socialism), then you, you see, are one of the causers and one of the spreaders of the fears that are causing all of the sickening diseases that already drown, choke, strangle, and kill the dreams, hopes, the plans, blueprints, and struggles, of the billion that now stagger sickly around and about.

Your friend,
WOODY GUTHRIE

My Job as a Poet

My job as a poet as I know it
Is easy
But it's hard
Easiest and the hardest one job

[68]

I guess I ever did tackle
My job as a poet
Is the same as suet is suet
Same as a shoat is a shote
And a goat likes to smell it
Like a poet likes to tell it
And a dreamer likes to scream a dream
Just like my woman likes to spill cream
And I like to get naked and roll
My job as a poet
Is the funniest one job I ever took on
I love my job as a poet
It gets me in and out real easy
Women go for it
Girls run and fall and roll for it
Men get mixed up about it
Most guys don't know what to do about it
Most men hate every poet they see
Because most poets hate most every man they see
And this makes me a poet
The world has already built me a legend
And several yarns, tales and stories about me
True, untrue, halftrue, not true,
Almost true, nearly true, not quite true,
Every flavor of gossip and lip lapping you ever heard
This more than anything else
Is what makes me a poet in the folking field
I am a folking poet and glad to show it
As a cow is to meow and a cat is to show it
I love my job of being your poet
Because I can drink your liquor and your beer
And drink your good wine and your wife's blood
And call it a poem and say I'll mention your name in my
     poems
And you ask me to sleep with your daughters and your wives
And to eat at your tables and your boards

Just so long as I mention your name in my next book of poems
Just so I write down your name in my next booklette of songs
    and fulk ballads
Just so I write down your name
You beat everybody else up with your fists, but you skip me
    saying
Will I please please please take all of your belongings and
Will I please mention your name in my next poem.
        don't you turn out to be a poet and come and sleep
            with my wife
        all of my groceries and meats?
        mention my name in your next book of poems
            and fulksongs?

June 5, 1947

How to Make Up a Balladsong and Get Away With It

So far I've not been able to tell the difference between a folk song and a ballad.

But for now, let us say that a ballad always tells you a story about something that happens to somebody somewhere.

A folk song might not tell you a whole story, but tells you what you think about some person, some question, or about some political issue.

    I'm gonna marry you, Sally Ann
    I'm gonna marry you quick as I can

Now, if you see a folk song that tells you, I'm gonna marry you quick as I can, and the very next words tell:

    Woodpecker peckin'
    And the bark a flyin'

>   Old folks a huggin'
>   And the kids a cryin'—

you see, that's a story. It's a tale, it's telling you something that's happening to several people.

The first verse didn't tell you anything that was happening, but it did tell you that I was hoping and thinking, desiring, and craving to marry you quick as I possibly can.

The song, "Sally Ann," you see, is partly a ballad telling you a little story, and partly a folk song telling you what's going on in my head.

You'll run onto all kinds of songs and ballads which are fullblood, halfbreed, one-quarter breed, eighth, sixteenth, thirty-second and all down the line.

There's not any more real difference between a folk song and a pure ballad than there is between a street and an avenue.

For my own use, I've always just called a song a song. I didn't even hear the word "ballad" nor the word "folk," well, till I hit New York in the snow of '41.

And, well, to be right honest with you, I've been one of the mixed-uppest men out of all the others all the way around this planet.

A song was just a song to me. I never even heard any song called a folk song.

After all, every song is a song by the folks and for the folks. I don't recall ever writing any songs for cows, chickens, fish, monkeys, nor wild animals of any kind.

In my own mind, a song is just a song.

Funny song, sad song, dancey song, story song. Song to set and listen to. Song to make you work easier. Question song. Puzzle song, riddle song, blues song, ragtime song, waltzing song, drinking song, and all other kinds of songs.

Every song that is liked by the folks is said to be a popular song. The very word "popular" means "liked by the people." So, you see, a song can be old as a hug in the trees and still be "popular" and "liked by the people." That word "pop tune" does not mean that your pop song just came out last week. Lots of new tunes are not popular with the people, and lots of new tunes will be sung and loved by all of us a thousand years from now.

Questions, please:

Where will I get my ideas to write my songs and ballads? Answer to that is:

Everywhere you look, out of books, magazines, daily papers, at the movies, along the streets, riding buses or trains, even flying along in an airplane, or in bed at night, anywhere.

Always keep your pencil and paper handy to jot down little and big ideas.

How will my ideas come to me?

Answer:

Ideas will come so fast that you won't be able to finish all of them.

I see new ideas in every book I read, a history book gives me all kinds of ideas for writing history songs, such as this one:

Biggest Thing

I read in the papers about wrecks, accidents, fires, floods, droughts, hurricanes, cyclones, rapings, killings, and family squabbles, lovers' troubles, rackets and racketeers, gangster fights, bad houses, slum diseases, tragedies of all kind, such as train, plane, ship, car wrecks. Explosions. All kinds of disasters.

Any event which takes away the lives of human beings, I try to write a song about what caused it to happen and how we can all try to keep such a thing from happening again.

Like that coal dust explosion that blew up the number five mine shaft in Centralia, and took away a hundred some men.

Goodbye Centralia

Most songs that last the longest are the ballads that tell you a story about the news of the day.

I can't invent the news every day. Nobody can. But I can do my little job which is to fix the day's news up to where you can sing it. You'll remember it lots plainer if I can make it easy for you to sing the daily news at your job or else at your play hours.

Such as the Nazi torpedo that blew up this famous American ship before we declared war on Hitler and Mussolini:

The Reuben James

Or this one I made up so's you wouldn't be forgetting what happened to this famous Negro soldier less than three hours after he got his Honorable Discharge down in Atlanta, Georgia.

Isaac Woodard

(I sung this Isaac Woodard song in the Lewisohn Stadium one night for more than 36,000 people, and I got the loudest applause I've ever got in my whole life. This song is a long song, but most of the action is told in Isaac's own words. I made this ballad up because we'll need lots of songs like this one before we win our fight for racial equality in our big free United States.)

Pete Seeger and myself sang some of our protest songs one night down at the meeting hall of the Tenant Farmer's Union Hall in Oklahoma City, where Bob and Ma Woods made some talks and answered all kinds of questions. A gang of toughies dressed up like workers came down to start a fight and bust up our meeting. I read a little article there about how a gang of thuggers had carried a tenant farmer union girl out and hung her up in an old log shack where they tore off her clothes and whipped her with straps and things.

Bob Wood told me that our good music actually tamed

down this gang of thugs and kept a big fight from breaking out. I sat up most of the night using Ma's little portable typewriter and I wrote up this song to the tune of "Redwing" to tell all of you union busters how I felt about you and your gospel of hate. I wrote this song that night.

(I've seen several million men, women, and boys and girls march in labor strikes and parades while they sang this one out):

Union Maid

If you like to play music and sing, you can write songs, if you try.

But writing songs is not an easy job, it's not a pushover.

You'll find out before very long just how hard the job is.

A good writer of good songs ought to read all kinds of books, pamphlets, papers, magazines, that you can lay your hands on.

You ought to read good books in the field of nature and natural history, specially, I'd say, *The Origin of Species* and *The Descent of Man* by Charles Darwin. Darwin tells a million little real-life stories that happen every day in the world of bugs, birds, animals of all kinds, and how man has worked and fought his way up to be the boss over every critter and varmit on this planet earth.

I've read lots of books on biology, botany, zoology, germology, modern science, and watched ten million kinds of germs and cells and plasms fight and eat one another up, under a microscope.

I've written lots of songs and poems that go to show you that the germs, plasms, bugs, bees, birds, monkeys, all work, and fight and make love and breed, and have big wars and peace dances just like us humans do.

A poem or a song that tells about any kind of a fight will catch most every eye that can read.

A song or poem that tells about a love affair, legal or illegal, will catch most every eye and ear that can hear.

The fight can be a fight that leads up to a love affair, or your song can tell about how a love affair led up to a fight. Love affairs and fights are all tangled up like dry leaves in a spider web.

Your fight can be one that gets two lovers together, all paired and mated. Then you can go on to make up more songs about how much working and slaving and fighting it takes to see our pair of lovers build them up a home to feed and to clothe and to keep their kids in out of the weather.

A flat blue million songs have already been written and sung about the fight you've got to put up to keep your mouths half fed and your house and home going.

1. Single Girl Blues
2. Two Hungry Babies
3. Starving Family Blues
4. Leaky Roof Blues
5. No Money Blues
6. The Drunken Father
7. The Frozen Orphan
8. The Drunk Mother
9. Wish I Was Single Again
10. Holey Stockin' Blues
11. No Rent Blues
12. No Job Blues
14. Parents' Lament
15. Crowded Room Blues
16. GI Loan Blues
17. Hock Shop Rag
18. Pawn Shop Polka
19. Bucket Shop Waltz
20. Trifling Husband
21. Trifling Wife

22. Trifling Sweetie
23. Jealous Father
24. Jealous Mother
25. Daggery Knife
26. Oily Gun Rag
27. Dead Widow
28. Dead Bachelor
29. Stabbing at Home
30. Starved Relatives
31. Hungry Heart Blues
32. No Job Moan
33. Down Payment Scream
34. Dollar Down Struggle
35. The Collector Man
36. The Dying Collector
37. The Dead Collector
38. Mortgage Day Blues
39. Rent Day Shuttle
40. Gas Bill Scuttle
41. Light Bill Runaway
42. High Price Gallop
43. Low Pay Work Hand
44. Inflation Struggle
45. Banker Man Blues
46. The Banker Man
47. The Hurt Banker
48. The Landlord
49. The Dying Landlord
50. That Dead Landlord
51. Hungry Baby Blues
52. Empty Bottle Lament
53. No Heat Weeper
54. Coldwater Flat Blues
55. No Coal Moan
56. No Oil Cry

57. Chilly Fever Shivver
58. Band Cold Blues
59. Cold Room Blues
60. Holey Roof Breakdown
61. Mean Boss Ballad
62. Mean Old Judge Blues
63. Gone Woman Blues
64. Gone Man Blues
65. Sickly Woman Blues
66. Sick Man Moan
67. Headache for Breakfast
68. Pellagra for Dinner
69. Malaria for Supper
70. Join the Union
71. Go and Join the Union
72. Go Down and Join the Union
73. Go Up and Sign Up
74. Union's My Religion
75. Union's My Savior
76. Union Pay
77. Union Day
78. Union Way
79. Union Man
80. Union Boy
81. Union Girl
82. Union Woman
83. Union Saved Me
84. Scabs in My Factory
85. Scabs in My Job
86. Scabs in My Place
87. Scabs in My Hair
88. Scabs in My Eyes
89. Scabs in My Bed
90. Scabs in My Bread
91. Shoo Scabby Shoo

129. High Peppy Hepper
130. Loud Shouting Whooper
131. Freedom Jitterbug
132. Groove Juice Rider
133. Dinner Pail Workster
134. New Found Good Time
135. Rent Paid Blues
136. Good Shoe Joke
137. Good Stockin Snicker
138. I Love Folks
139. Folks Loves Me
140. Union Heated Sweetie
141. The Hot Union Kiss
142. These Burnt Union Hugs
143. Oh, My Union
144. Yes, My Union
145. My World Union
146. Union Home
147. Union Mattress
148. Union Bed Spring
149. Union Baby
150. Union Children.

Just the idea of the title for your song is more than half of the battle to catch your ballad.

I've got thousands of titles laid away like postal saving bonds. I spend hours and hours just writing down my ideas for titles to my songs.

> For wine or beer my balladeer
> Sings wild tales for my ladies here
> For gin and rum my lady comes
> And dances with her hip bones
> And dances with a belly rub
> And dances out the story told

O honey bun
Thy belly rubid
Is more to me
Than
Folksong sung
O honey bell
Thy slick hip helt
Means more to me
Th'n ballad yell'd

If you've not seen my belly warsh,
    if you've not seen my deucy
    dew,
If you've not seen my douchey
    warsh
I'll show it to you now, now,
I'll show you how it goes

                                    and went bent

   I jump up late of nights and grab somebody's pencil and
somebody's paper and write down just the title line to some
balladsong on the upper end of a blank sheet of paper and
jump out of some other bed several years later and set down
the words to that ballad idea that hit me several beds ago.
You've got to be financially able to pay for a large number of
beds if you have the least notion of ever being any kind of a
folkballadsong maker.
   I can look out here through my window right now and see
some hard-working man using a post hole digger to dig a
post hole. He digs his hole down in the green grass in my
neighbor's yard and the grass hangs all around the edges
and rims and sides of his hole for his post. He pours a can
of water down into his hole to make his digger thing slide

easier and to grab the mud out a lot faster. He looks at the grass growing all around his hole and it makes him see thoughts and hot visions about that woman he'sa loving with. Can you your ownself take this post hole diggerman idea from here and make up a song about it? You can use any kind of a rhythm beat from a fast sexy boogy beat on over to a slower kind of a spiritual hoping song about the woman he's got or about the one that he keeps on looking for.

Your songs and your ballads, just like every other kind of a job of work you'll ever do, will be just as good as the number of days and months and weeks and years that you put in as a song and a ballad maker.

You are always on the job, there is no let-up, no rest, no vacation for you and for the ballad maker in you. You are always your own boss, you and all of your people around your world here. You'll keep going, always looking, always fishing, always catching some more of your old or new ideas.

Every step you step you'll be hunting for more ballad ideas. You have to go just like the newsreel camera crew goes, or like the news reporter folk, or like the artist always goes to the real place where people are living through the things your song is all about. Sometimes I come right out and tell people I'm trying to make some ballads out of their strugglings and other times I talk to them and get them to tell me (by hook or crook) what I want to know from them and finish my ballads off in a hotel room, on some train, in a truck cab, or down alongside of some road.

If my ballads are to be of a kind where I have to take sides with a poltical issue or an argument along economic lines, where policemen are around in very large numbers, then I do all my going, asking, talking, and looking around· in plain sight and most of my ballad carving hid off and out someplace where no privvy-eyed FBI can see me. And because this FBI does brand all of your best songs, poems, pictures, ballads, dances, prances, stances and romances as being too muchly political, then, well, you just have to learn how to tell the FBI folks to go straight to hell and never be so afraid of them as to run any direction on your compass to hide from them neither before nor after you've made your ballads about the true history of the lives of the people around you. Your ballads will be lots better and sound lots plainer and clearer when you stop all kinds of hiding, even hiding from your own people or from your ownself.

After some few years in the hottest part of the everyday battle of your working people to win for their ownselves and their own loved ones a better life, then your senses will get to be so sharp and so keen that you can turn through the pages of any earthly book and find another history ballad to make from every page. And your ballad you make out of these pages of written history will be every bit as clear and as fair and as honest and as useful to my human race as any ballad you've ever made up from walking and from talking to fighters out along my very front line. Your own book of your own ballads will be printed and bound up into another kind of a history book just as useful and as usable as any book so far ever printed.

The Tune
To Use With the
Words to Your Ballads.

Most generally this idea for your tune will come to you long before the work came.

Like my tunes come to me for my ballads.

I decide on which mixture of a tune to use and then I find it about a dozen times easier to herd my words into my tune I've already built for them.

I never waste my high-priced time by asking or even wondering in the least whether I've heard my tune in whole or in part before. There are ten million ways of changing any tune around to make it sound like my own. I can sing a high note instead of a low note or a harmony note for a melody note and put in a slow note for several fast ones, or put in several fast ones for a slow one, and shuffle my rests and my pauses around here and yonder and be able to make the bottom idea of any tune fit my new ballad idea.

I love most, I guess, and confess to find my own ways in my own balladsongs to speak up, to speak out what's rambling around in my own mind. I love to protest about things that I see need protesting against, like all the sorry sad situations I can plainly see, like mobbing, and lynching, and bombing, and burning and killing, all of which are caused when you let yourself get afraid of any shape, any form, any flavor, any kind of racial hatred. I never would have craved like I did to write so many balladsongs, anyhow, if I'd not been able to tell you what I think is wrong with this world we're living in.

March 8, 1948

Anthropology

Some young wife come here to my house tonight with her husband. He goes to some college here in town and takes up the study of lost causes.

His wife said that she was over taking a course in anthropology. I didn't want to act like I didn't know what that stuff is. So I just kept quiet.

I always did keep quiet when I don't know what something is. I'd say that this keeps my lips latched up about three fourths of the time. And I most generally tear loose to talk later on about something which I'm sure not very certain about.

Anthro. Anthro. Pologizing. Pologizing to the Anthroes? For what?

Why pologize to them?

What did I do to them to make them sore? What did she? She had all of the looks of a nice broadheaded young wife. How could she make these anthroes so mad at her? Maybe they'd ought to switch it all around and make the anthroes apologize to the wife.

I heard a man one day tell about an ape that he called an anthro ape. Anthro Ape. Anthroe Apes.

Maybe she works on them Anthroed Apes.

Maybe she puts them together. Putting Apes back together.

That sounds like a mighty fine kind of a job if you can really get out and work at it and get paid for it.

Putting all kinds of apes back together. To study the stones and rock formations in the apes' skulls. There's going to be a big plenty of skulls here in New York's rocks if we let our military apers march us off into the barditch of this atomic war.

Her husband had two friends along with him. They knew my wife from her kidhood days and parks. They wanted to play a game of chess with my chessfellers here in my kitchen tonight, but I gave them my chess set and my chessmen and my chessboard and told them to go somewhere else to play. So, my wife went out with them somewhere to have a few minutes of gossip about all of their babies coming. Babies are better to talk about than to try to put an ape back together.

Let's all take a big trip and go around to all the jailhouses, insane asylums, old poorhouses, and whorehouses, and prisons and side streets and vacant lots and weed patches, and try to put the people back together again. To hell with them apes. They can patch up their own histories. Humans can't. They need patching up and booting.

May 31, 1949

Bits and Snatches

Oh, some parts of this state are right awful hilly but then again some of it's awful badly flat or awful good. The hilly parts ain't near as flat as the flat parts are. Only thing wrong with this state's the people that own it. What I'd really like to be able to figure out is where did they git it? Bad year comes and the weather gets your crops. Good years the landlord gets them. Landlord says I owe him some money just for being born into his world here that he stole off from me there.

A girl's face in the window of a blue sedan
As she bit her lip and looked out for her man
The morning's early sun is in your eyes
As you look at something yonder in the skies
And you lick your lips and hold your steering wheel
I guess I know almost just how you feel
As you shoot your eyes on the windows of this train
And look for the face that planted all of your grain.

A cat on a chicken coop scratches his chin
Waits for a train load of eggs to roll in.

Old rotten barn. Big young new barn.
Old fell down house. Right big new house.
Good rich dirt. Then some wore out land.
But the land can get made new again like a man.
And if you're going to get made new you got to plan.

Truckload of gravel going somewhere to spill
"I'm a good truck driver. Just cain't pay my bill!"

I wouldn't say that I'm a part of this dirt but then I guess I am. Fast as I go out and get dirty all over my woman makes me take some soapy water and wash it all off. Now if I was made out of this dirt like you say I am, what makes it come loose from me so easy with a little soap and water? So I stand here on this dirt. And I walk on dirt. And I do my work here on this dirt. And I dig in it and move it all around every-where. Anywhere I want to. I laid a couple of women down on it and laid two wives down in it. And I still stand up here above it and look down at it. If I am made of dirt it's sure dirt on the move because I'm always on the hump and the go all the time.

I'm like this whole country on the blow and on the go.
I'm like this whole country in the sun and in the snow
I'm like this whole country on the trust and on the bust
I'm like this whole country every minute of the day
On the blow and on the go in the sun and in the snow
On the trust and on the bust every minute of the day.

My wife says the main reason why she likes me is because I'm as crazy as a turkey gobbler.

High prices. You talk about high prices. I went into my store to buy some eggs and the man charged me fifty-nine cents for a dozen. I went back in a week later and he stuck me sixty-four cents. I bought a dozen the third week and he charged mè seventy-three cents. And so I went in to buy a dozen this morning. And he was there. And he had his money up on his shelf and his eggs in the cash register.

Last night I got to Akron a right good rubber town
On the Cuyahoga river that runs from Cleveland down
I sung at the Akron Armory, a big nice dirty hall,
And I never met better people in all of my life before.

I tried to write a song about the Columbia river and all of the five tributaries, the Snake river, Hood river, Willamette, Yakima river, and the Klickitat. Well, all I could sing was:

That Columbia river takes them all to the ocean blue
That Columbia river takes them all to the ocean blue

That Columbia river takes them all to the ocean blue
Snake. Hood. Willamette. Yakima. An' Klickitat, too.

Let's rake it up and shake it up and go.
Wake up blue and snap down on some hot meat.
You know I'd shovel a mile of manure with my nose just to
get to sniff at the hair on your skin.
This train stops at Frost Bite, Rabbit Track, Pump Handle,
Mary's Veil, Prospect Gap, Bitter Sprout, Hang Down, Corn
Shock, Ditty Wa Ditty and Coffin Corners on its way to
Wormy Hill.
This is that time of the year when birds fly down
And pick up seeds with people off of the ground.

I know this is me doing this here. I know it. I know this
is me here. I know I'm tickling you to death and I'm so glad
about it that I'm just a bubbling. I know this is me here you
don't have to tell me. This is me.
Sundown! Sunnnnndowwnnn!
Looky! Looky! Look!
Looky yonder where that fireball's gone!
    Goodbye to old Akron goodbye for a while
    I'm leaving you now crost a many a sad mile.
No man in the world looks at you like a railroad conductor.
    Grab your stuff
    And hold your seats
    I'm sellin' sandwitches
    Jesus couldn't eat.
                    You see what Cleveland
                    Has done done to me
                    How broke and how lonesome
                    A good man can be.

Oh there's fog on the window of my train
Oh there's fog fog a fogging in my brain

Come Smell of me now

woody Guthrie

1951

I hit that hotel on the run
And they rolled me for my mun
Yes! There's fog on the window of my train.
  I got the screws put to me
   The skids slid under me
    Got the old greasy finger
     Got the sheet yanked out from under me
      Somebody beat me there ahead of time
  I got the grease eased to me easy
   And I got my traveling papers
    And they gimme my walking gear
    And they oozed me over lightly
     I think I got horn swoggled
      Pushed out got the jump on me
       That's how come I'm like I am
This day's gonna be my new burial day
Kill old Jim Crow and lay him away
This day's a-gonna see a new union sun
Jim Crow and poll tax and slavery'll be gone.
  An' It's a gonna rainnnn rainnn
  An' it's a gonna rainnnnnnnnnnnnnn
  An' it won't be waterrrrrrrrrrrrr
  But fire. Next time.
You buy 'em an' sell 'em, 'cause I c'n 'ford ta sell more'n
you c'n 'ford ta buy.
  I don't know why it is but I feel about half of the time
like I'd ought to be everywhere else in the world except right
here where I am.

Reckless Talk

Chorus: Oh, you see what your reckless talk can do?
         Don't you see what your reckless talk can do?

You can see what your reckless talk can do
I don't want no reckless talk from you!

There is a ship that sails the ocean blue. (three times)
And her name I cannot tell to you.
(Chorus)
When you hear of a ship and a crew done gone. (three
times)
See what your rattling tongue has done!
(Chorus)
That ocean's dark and the ocean's cold. (three times)
So don't rattle off everything you know.
(Chorus)
A clattering tongue is an awful thing. (three times)
When you think of the sorrow it might bring.
(Chorus)
The least little word that you might say. (three times)
Might send a ship to a watery grave.
(Chorus)
Us boys that ride this ocean blue. (three times)
We don't want no reckless talk from you.

Born to Win

I had my fun and my troubles
I had my hard luck and blues
Been up and been down and been sober and drunk
But I know that I'm not born to lose.

Chorus: Born to win. I know I'm born to win.
           It's a funny old world that I am in.
           I'll fight to change it like it ought to be.
           Born to win. I know I'm born to win.

I had women all kinds and all colors
In every land where I have been
I saw all the people in trouble like me
And I know that we're not born to lose.

(Chorus)

You robbed us and beat us and bled us.
You worked us and paid us like slaves.
I know we're all born to work and to fight
And to win or go down in our grave.

(Chorus)

The maddest I've been in my whole life was when I rode on a troopship with more than three thousand men headed for France and we got about half way out on the ocean and a big storm come up. The ship rocked and rolled and made a lot of us sick. We hadn't been across before. We turned on our radio and a song blubbered out over the loudspeaker, "Born to Lose!" Ain't that some hell of a damned song for the United States Army to have poked down its throat on its way into a battle?

I couldn't rest easy till I run and grabbed my pencil and wrote this one down. "Born to Win."

My Dear Mr. Truman

BROOKLYN, NEW YORK
JULY 31, 1949

MY DEAR MR. TRUMAN:

If you even so much as lay a small claim to be a human with a brain, a soul, a heart, a mind, a feeling you could call the warmth of the blood of man, please, good sir, take a good look at these bills you are signing to make more high explosives to blow us all off the map. Your face will look a whole lot blanker if the little atoms blow our world away and all of your pals and kinfolks along with the rest of us.

I'm not ready to blow just yet.

Your old buddy,
Woody Guthrie

Us Kids

We took thirty-six ships, freighters and tankers, from the Rock of Gib. to the Island of Sicily, town called Palermo, on this certain night in '44. Nazi torpedoes fired six of our ships just before we got to the docks. I could feel the hot heat from the blazing ships while we stood along our railings and listened to the lost crewmen, GI's, gunboys and officers.

Jimmy Longhi, Cisco Houston and myself walked ashore with a pair of guitars and a little flatback Gibson mandolin. Longhi was just getting his first few blisters on his fingers from the heat of rough strings on his first guitar, Jim wore the jacket and apron of an officer's messman part of his time on board the *William B. Travis* (we nicknamed the *Travis* the "Willy Bee"), and while he was not on duty as a feeder of officers, Jimmy read in his bunk or out on the open deck from the pages of several leather smelling law books. He was studying to "try to pass the bar." Jim was one glad man when he saw that our Willy Bee had noosed up at a Sicilian port, because he had learned how to talk good fast clear Italian from his father who was a union organizer down around the New York waterfront.

Cisco was an older hand at playing chords on the guitar,

but he could not talk more than a dozen or so Italian words which he'd picked up just imitating Italians when he'd hear them. Cisco had always been in some spot of the show game, on some kind of a platform all of his on and off hours. He was a singer with a WPA bunch out around Los Angeles. He traveled around to the Federal Migratory Worker camps and put on union skits, songs, and shows with Will Geer, Herta Ware, assorted movie stars and me. Cisco and Jimmy were near the same age, I think, about twenty-four. I was lots older and grayer in the head, I was thirty-two.

We saw the pile of garbage that was still named Palermo. Four hundred thousand folks used to live here under Mussolini's Fascists, Hitler's Nazis, then under the Allies of all kinds. The curfew was on, and we were there at the wrong hours. It was against the law for us to be out on the streets. We didn't want to get arrested and fined all of our ship's wages, so we steered to the outer parts of Palermo, and climbed up the side of a high mountain eight miles till we hit a little peasant town by the name of Altofonte. Jimmy told us that Altofonte meant high ground, high place or high lookout. High something.

We made lots of friends awful fast, traipsing and singing around the streets and alleyways of Altofonte. Gangs of kids danced all around us and joked in Italiano while we played and sung. They showed us a barber shop where a little shoeshine boy had knelt down to shine the boots of fourteen Nazi troopers, and instead of pulling the stopper out of his polish bottle, he pulled the pin out of a hand grenade that killed everybody in the shop. Another building they showed us where three or four boys and girls had stolen bars of soap from the Allies and hid them down in the cellar of a girly house. The bars of soap turned out to be bars of nitro hotstuff, and the Nazis hadn't any sooner dropped the copper pennies down into the hands of the boys and girls than, *whinggg*, and the place went up, and then down into a pile

[93]

of loose dusty trash. The bodies of the girls and the men sticking together in their wrecked beds made quite a sight to see.

These kids took up with us first. They asked us all kinds of questions, looked us up and down good and proper, they said that they trusted us because we were merchant seamen, and not soldiers of any breed. They trusted us more because they liked our singing and our music. They took us around to several houses where we had some purple thick wine, some bread, some macaroni, and some talks with the older folks. They saw to it that several beautiful girls in their early and late twenties took us on a looking tour down along the side of the mountain through some wild lemon trees, fig orchards, grapevines several hundred years old.

"Do not peek up eny watch."

"No fountan panz."

"Noe. Noe. Nawthing. Peek up nawthing. No rifles, no bulleets, no wallet, no pockeetbook, no gold ring, see? Savvy? No peek up nawthing. See?"

"Hey. Looky. Joe."

"She got wire, see? Rope? String. You poola stringa, she go blooom. Beeg mountain boom up. TNT. See?"

By waving, dancing, motions of every kind they made Cisco and me savvy. Don't pick up anything.

A big cloud of rotten-looking dust jumped up towards the sky about ten miles out, down and across a deep grape and orchard valley. It shook the whole mountain under my feet. I'd never heard nor seen any such an explosion or noise in my whole life to match the roar of this one. The kids stood around us and winked, nodded their heads and made us see what they were getting at.

"What's that?" Cisco asked a gang farther up the hill from me.

"Ammoneesha doomp."

"Who dunnit?" I asked them.

"Ohhhh. Boys. Girls, Keedsa."

"Musta beena whole train loada th' stuff went up," I said.

"Hoonderd tranfool," one girl smiled out under a fig stem. She pooched her lips up like she felt glad to see the dump blow up. "Tan, feefteen beega boatfool. Heetlair werrk two three years pile da beeg ammonish oop. We let Heetlair go werk, see?" She snapped her fingers down at her knee and laughed so quiet that it didn't even shake a cactus thorn.

The kids all over the mountain done dances and sung songs to imitate the sound of the explosion. Cisco grunted somewhere in the vineyard. Jimmy made a sound like a cannon booming. I did the same.

I made a walk down the hill a ways and, somehow, got lost from the other folks. I smoked a cigaret and looked all around at the old trees, cactus apples, knotty lemons, twisted grapevines the size of my arm at my elbow. I started to reach down and pick up a brass clip of ten or fifteen bullets, thinking I'd carry them back and give them to the peasants in the village. Three or four green apricots, figs, clods of dirt, small-size rocks and other objects whizzed all around my head and knocked up the dirt around my feet. I saw two or three of the kids prance out from behind clumps of bushes, weeds, old rockwalls, haystacks, cactus patches. They all shook their heads. "Naww. Noooeee. Noooee. No peek oopa, Joe. Tummy tum tum. Tumma tumtum. Rummy dum dum. Noe. Noe. Noe."

I was just standing there looking at the thousands of fine brassy polished bullets laying all around in some short grass on a hot sunny spot when I heard Jimmy yell from the wild vines farther around the mountain.

"Hi. Cisssco. Woody. C'mon. Kids are gonna show us where the Nazis let all of their old letters pile up when they ran out!"

"Cominnn'," Cisco yelled from somewhere with his mouth chock full of cactus apple seeds that dripped down all over his clean shirt while he tried to answer. "Mighty perty cactus apples they gotta 'roun' here. Might perty wimmen ta help y' pick 'em."

"Shore are!" I was yelling and walking up towards Jimmy and his bunch. "Mighty fine-lookin' grape vines, ta boot. I allus did crave ta be a big ole grapey vine summers on th' sunnyslope uv sum pergressiv mount'n, summers."

"We've got to be getting back to our sweet Willy Bee!" Jimmy hollered out. "Now, Cisco, you and Woody know very good and well that you'd lots rather to be back there walking up and down that Willy Bee deck than out here chasing around half wild on the lazy side of some Sicilian mountain. Git a wiggle on. These kids know where a whole Nazi camp is. I mean, a camp the Nazis left out from so fast they didn't even take their papers and pencils."

I walked up to Jimmy's herd of boys and girls. "Pens an' pencils. Huhmm. Reminds me. Did I lose my Parker Fifty-One? Nope. Gottit. Hyere 'tiz." I had to wait about a minute till Cisco and his guides caught up to us. I touched my pen point to the skin on my arm to see if it had any ink left in it. I drew a funny looking cartoon of Mussolini in the palm of my hand. When I wiggled my fingers, the mouth would fly open and talk like Musso. A little girl held out her hand for one of the same tattoos of Mussy. A little boy waited with his sleeves rolled up to his armpit. Then another one. I drew not less than twenty-five, and closer to fifty, of these crazy faces of Mussolini and Hitler on the arms of the boys and girls. Some stood still, some walked along slow and easy with us to show us the way to the camp the Nazis had hauled tail from.

The camp was down in a low place. A little stream of clear water trickled through under some shortneck trees. An old watermill rockhouse had been the head office, with tents tossed up all around. Then something had happened, and they all took off in such a fast run that they left postcards, letters, pictures, cigars, cigarets, books, matches, bullets, guns, grenades and everything else you carry to be a big high powered soldier. Jimmy told Cisco and me, "Somebody set fire to their bullet wagon. Somebody blew up three of their gasoline trucks. Somebody flurked up their radio wires. Somebody let the air out of their tires. Know who it was?"

"Guess it very easy." Cisco dug around in an old pile of letters and family photos thrown and scattered everywhere amongst the rot of the sewage along the creek banks. "Kids?"

"Yeahhp." Jimmy was loading his arms full of bullets, letters, pin-up girls, Nazi propaganda superman books, pamphlets, calendars and other articles of warfare. "Kids."

I was taking on a waterline load of the same stuff. I looked at the kids kicking and digging all in under the trees. I asked them, "Say, has this stuff gotta big boom on th' end uvvit?" They just smiled and said, "Joe, thessa fascista, thessa Nazi fella, he roon way fast, like thees. Theees. No tam left for to tie beeg boom on. See? 'Stan'?"

"Yeah." I loaded my arms, my pockets, my pants legs, everything. I had enough war souvenirs to give to half of Coney Island when I got back home. I could study the Nazi and the Fascist morale by reading their letters and postcards home. "Who'd ya say 'twas that chais'd th' Natzees outta hyere sa dern fast? Th' Allies? Th' partysans? Th' Red Army? Who wuzzit?"

Some little feller way back off out in the bowjack weeds spoke up sort of half weary, half laughing, and said, "Eet wass not eny of them. Ha. Eet wass jusst uss keeds."

Another one said, "I giff to the Nazis pishy vino. I sell to the Fascist poison beer. I naver leave heem asleep. I no let heem geet weeth girrrl, see? I roona heema ploomba craze! Me. Ha. Uss keeds."

"Usss keeds." Jimmy pounding his own chest. "Uss keeds," Cisco went into a wild whooping peace dance. And I walked back down towards the little trail that looked down over the Palermo harbor and said, "Our Willy Bee's a-waitin' f'r uss kids. Gotta go."

Jimmy, Cisco and myself had on such a heavy load of souvenirs that we couldn't even play nor sing much on our way back to the boat.

That same night, pulling out of Palermo with a full cargo of memories about "uss keeds," the Willy Bee ran into the hot firey end of a Nazi torpedo.

June 8, 1948

Censors and You and Me

Suggytit what I could tell you
If this censor wasn't here
Would raise your hide, and melt your wax,
It'd coil your hair,
It'd burn your ear,
Them censor folks get paid
For stopping me from telling you
The ways I feel
Sweet Babe,
When I feel just like I feel
Towards you
Right here
Right now
Censors
And you
And me
Somebody's gotta be tossed out and it ain't
        you and it ain't me.
So
Hoonthellizzit?

Dear Prostitute:

I, in my day and time, was forced by the fun of the thing, and by the heat of my feelings, to spend with you

Our thirty-one nights and days,

Some few mornings, afternoons, odd hours, as we met up at all of those odd places,

The rotten shack in the Texas boomtown, and told you that I loved your body, but hated your old rotty shack and your old crummy mattress.

I loved you and I told you so, yes, even before I climbed over on top of your belly and before I slid my hot pecker in at your juicy place. I told you I' ridd you till you felt so good that you would give me a

Drink of your bitter bottle

And pay me to stay with you

Just so you could hold the rumps of my hips in your hand and wiggle your whole body, Honey Sweet, and roll, and squirm,

And pooch it out slick, hot, wide open, oozing that sweet blistery juice of love's own creating, dripping down in the folded hot skin between those proud kicky legs of yours.

I didn't catch any disease from you, and your skin and hair and eyes have changed off to every color while my lips and my tongue went over you. I came to you in love to offer you myself to get you out of your trap.

But my work took me on away from you in other directions. I hated the system of pussy and penis for profit, but this was not anywhere in you, nor in your actions.

I slack my speed today

To tell you I wish my tickly pecker could shoot a whole
army up in the hills of your belly to march out right this very
hour and kill this whole blackmarket system that lays us in
our beds of chancred hate

For a penny or two clear profit.

Kids Can Squawl

Kids can squawl
And kids can bawl
As long as the ants pack hayseeds
I like a kid that bawls real loud
And grows up a big loud lung
To walk up to some pizzeldyasst Washington Office
And yell out so loud
Up and down them crackly halls
That they pass five or six laws that minute
By gollies
To give my kid whatever the heck he's yelling for.

June 10, 1949

This ain't nobody's birthday I can think of, is it, can you?
Gessnott.

Cisco Houston

Cisco Houston liked folk songs and folk ballads when he
first heard them. He heard a few odd records while he was
young and in his prime and taking active parts in learning
how to be an actor on the stage of the Pasadena Playhouse.

Ketchy You

Woody Guthrie   1951

He left this kind of life because he wanted things to hit him just a little bit harder, he wanted life to sort of knock some rougher and manlier lessons into his head. He took to the sealanes and to the searails at an early age and learned how to imitate every tongue and dialect of speech in every port and town the whole wide world around.

Cisco Houston is a champion at a lot of things. A champ swimmer, a champ runner, a champion actor, and a champion organizer of men into trade unions. Cisco likes hard-hitting songs and hard-hitting people. He likes to roam and to ramble, to walk, think, drink, and to talk with oil field roughnecks, timber slippers, mine crawlers, white collar city and town workers, with clerks, with folks on the ships, on trains, on fast-wheeling river barges, and to meet and to sing with people out in the bad kinds of weathers fighting for their rights to organize and to deal with the boss in a bunch.

He plays a big high-sounding guitar and is getting just about as good as they need to come. He's a man that likes most of all to meet new colors of people, newer colors of fields, hills, valleys, and new-looking mountains under every color of a sky. A man that rode the merchant boats all during the war and carried picket signs saying not to send your scrap iron and oil to Japan six or seven years back fighting the goons and the thugs out along the Ryan west coast country of Frisco, Seattle, Portland, and Los Angeles. He always takes the hard road to get where he is going to go, never the easy one, because the easy road isn't much to build up world union men along.

He sang with me in three trips and through three invasions in the merchant marine ships and we got torpedoed two times out of our three trips. I met a Negro boy that told me he had been torpedoed three times in one day up in the icey cold waters along our North Sea coasts, and so I stopped my bragging about my two torpedoes alongside of Cisco

this is how
Woody thinks he looks
+ HOW CISCO
THINK'S HE DRAWS

How Guthrie
really looks

By
Cisco

Houston who lost his brother, Slim, off the coast of Maine during the early days of the last world war, No. 2.

Cisco has been torpedoed enough times to make him one of the best. He's run into three tin fish, to be right exact about it. He has made several hundred records for Moe Asch of the Disc Company, been on several nationwide radio programs, as well as on BBC to Europe and to England and the OWI shortwave over the seas.

In my own mind, I see Cisco Houston as one of the manliest and best of our living crop of ballad and folksong singers. He is showman enough to make the grade and to hold any audience anywhere at anytime. He just finished a six week's run at Cafe Society downtown and the boss said he was going to rise and shine as high and as bright as any of the crop. I like Cisco as a man. I like him as a person, and as a fun-having, warmhearted, and likeable human being.

We are lucky, I think, to have a man like Cisco Houston booking out through our office at Peoples Artists and singing fighting and militant folk songs of social protest to the honor and to the dignity of the working man and woman everywhere across the humps and the falls of our country here. This is a big job and it is for big people with big faith in the humanly race everywhere.

I've heard Cisco sing with the Arabs, with the Mexicans, the Moors, the Sicilians, Irish, Scottish, Italians, Welsh, the Cubans, the Puerto Ricans, the Russians, Canadians, the Whites, the Blacks, the Browns, the tones and colors all in between. I say that when you hear Cisco's voice on these records you are going to like him the same way that my family likes him. The same way he likes you. Cisco is too young yet for me to putrefy about, but I prophecy that you'll be hearing him in the close and the near future days to come in albums of records for the Disc Company by himself, on his own, and with Blind Sonny Terry, Leadbelly, Peter Seeger, and along with me and my Barquero guitar.

I am positive that Cisco's choice of songs and ballads will always be from the deepest deeps of the heartblood that flows in such great pride and dignity from the lips and the tongues of the workers everywhere around this world today, working on and working on towards their one big union of the whole humanly race.

THIS IS THE BOSS

PUNCHIN' TH' CLOCK

BOSS WATCHES HAND WORK TILL SUNDOWN.

HAND GIVES BOSS
LOAF OF BREAD

HAND BUYS
LOAF OF BREAD

HANDS
KIDS
EAT
BREAD

CRIES
FOR
MORE

Prison Cell Dream

I dreamed last night that I got up
And walked out through these bars
Back to my wife and children and the folks I loved so well;
They all did laugh and dance and sing
To see me home again
Then I woke up here on my bunk all hot with aches and
   pains.

Chorus:

> THAT WAS A DREAM
> THAT WAS A DREAM
> THAT WAS A LONGTIME PRISON CELL DREAM

On my next night I dreamed I rode
On a hayride to the hills
We built a campfire big and bright and ate and drank our
   fill;
We all told jokes and stories
As we danced around the blaze;
I woke up in my cell agin with teardrops on my face.

(Chorus twice)

On my next night I dreamed I walked
To a dance hall here in town;
The lights they dimmed as I did spin the prettiest girl
   around;
She whispered hot words on my cheek
And I walked her home alone;

I woke up kissing my mattress, and my throat was burning
hot.

(Chorus twice)

December, 1949

I Drink and See Why

I drink and see why. So don't you bother to tell your friend
that you can't see why and don't see why.

And I overdrink for these same reasons that you overeat,
overdress, overtalk, overworry.

And why is it that you overly eat while I overly drink? Well,
since the both of us seem to be fishing out of the same
canoe, I'll tell you,

I'll tell you and then maybe you'll know

Maybe you'll know some of the why if not all of the why.

It's just like every other move and action in this world, it all
traces right back to my love life.

Not so much to the love life I have lived and will live, but
back to the love life that I'm just not living.

And back and back, and on back, to the love life I crave
and am not man enough nor genius nor poet nor husband
enough to get.

But, now, if I knew my woman better, or knew all women
better, then I'd know more what to say and what to do so
that she could know clear in herself all of my littlest and
my biggest cravings and desires.

But, you see, I'm not the expert, not the wisdom man enough

to always be able to pick out the right word to say when the time gets right.

And because, too, that I'm not smart enough to know this much about women.

I dream in my dreams and I see a husband and his wife going through certain acts and movements

Which I really think that every man and his wife had ought to live in and grow up and go through for the best outcome of her own dreams and of his the same

Which would fill the two of them so full of native and natural satisfaction that she wouldn't have the time nor the energy nor the power to turn her thoughts and thinking to restless things

And which would take the place of tobacco, snuff, dice, dominoes, cards, bridge, poker, snooker, blackjack, twenty-one, stud, bingo and bango, and replace in his mind closer dealings with his wife which would output and kick out all of these habits along with betting on the horses and on the rabbits chasing out away from the hounds

And would take the place of the bottle which I pay four or five times too much for, but which I don't set the price on, and so can't help

I know in my own head that if the correct passions of the lip and tongue are found by the wife and by the husband then these other outer and senselesser things will nearly or entirely pass out, fade away and die their natural death

Like they'd ought to, and the way they should.

I believe that if I find the mate that will find all of the answers to all of these little whispers of things unsaid that whichever kids do come out from our marriage will be kids happy enough and loved enough to not grow up at the age of ten, twelve or sixteen to grab a hammer, a rock, a brick-bat, a gun, a rifle, a pistol and say to the police and to the judge and to us the jury, I just felt a feeling come over me like I just had to kill somebody. Just to kill anybody. Anybody. It didn't matter who it was I killed. Just anybody that comes along.

These words aren't put in our kids' mouths by the kid himself nor herself. These thoughts and these words are planted in our kids by us dads and by us mamas. By us dads and mamas that never did have the nerve and the guts to find a love and a working life worth living. It is from our own restless unrest and cowardly silences that we grow full of such ideas that we can't even see our own kids in front of our eyes, much less teach our kids any kind of a thought to find a work, a job, a dignity that will fill us with the desires to go on working and living. And the hogtied and hobbled energies of our natural desires turn sour and turn rancid and break out loose and free from our chains in the forms and shapes of terrible crimes and nightmares all the way from muggings to rapings and murders. I see not one, but a dozen just such stories printed here every day all over the pages of my daily newspapers and magazines.

I think that this will always be the outcome of having to marry for the sake of moneys and deeds and titles of the ownership of real estate, and of land, and of houses, and of fields and pastures. Because if I, inside my own heart, know that my mate loves my bank account and not my own body nor my own self, or loves my deed and title instead of my works and my being, flesh and otherwise, well, then I'll never find that way to cause my partner to love me enough to make my hands and my mind work free and clear and healthy and honest. My doubt will turn into destruction. My fear will ferment into flat wine. My natural powers will turn to greeds of ten million deadly sorts and my works will be smeared and blotted out by my own false words and cowardly actions. This is the worst and most hidden and yet the plainest part of trying to live the life of a healthy human being under the planless plan of dog eat dog, every man for his own self, which we are dying out from trying to live under.

I'm not the only man nor the only kid nor the only woman nor the only girl that sees all of this and feels how plain and how clear and true it all is. I sometimes do think that I see the whole waste and drain dimmest of us all. I guess this is why I even take out the time to try to set some few words of my own feelings down here in print and thought.

I guess I wrote this down here just to try to show you that I do know this, do see it in all of these adult and kid crimes taking place in our street and alley and under our filthy bridge. It is not because there's something native and naturally wrong with us as humans, nor wrong with our kids as people. It's just something sad and dreary wrong with some of the outgrown pages of our leathered law books. Something blind in the old of us and something crippled in the dads and mamas of us. Something paralyzed and cramped in the worst and something chained and caged and locked and barred in the brightest of us.

It breaks out as an ulcer in me some of the time, then it jumps and takes the root of a cancer. It takes the visual form of skin sores and of running infections, as social and venereal diseases, as the v.d., the clap, the chancres, the syph, the paralysis, the jerking and frothing fits and spasms you call epileptic. I can see no matter how dizzy nor how sober I am that ninety some odd percent of my suffering and pain in every form is caused absolutely and positively by germs that get their killing start when I let down my bars of fighting resistance during my hours and minutes spent in fears and doubts and worries that I want our growing generation to find and to kill out by a unity and a warm friendliness that will reach from Kalamazoo to Alamogordo and to North and South Carolina, then on around this world.

May 28, 1947

Greasy String

From Woody Guthrie
To Irving Lerner

Seeing your film, *Banjo Pickin' Boy*, at the Preview Theater the other night has opened up all kinds of new hope in me. It come the closest to bringing the people their songs of any film, or book, or play, or picture painted, that I have ever seen.

I always did hope, somehow, that I would live long enough to see this very thing done with the camera and the mike, and all of the other tools of your trade. It was such a good feeling that I didn't know how to tell you there at the preview, nor down the elevator, nor even around the beer table later on. I was in the same state of mind that Joe Louis was in after he hung that shanty on Conn's jaw, about all I could say was, "Hello, folks," or something that didn't make much sense.

I've been thinking a lot about some kind of a film like *Banjo Pickin' Boy* for a long time. I've got it fairly well thought out in my own head, and will do my best to make you see it. Maybe you can see it in the form of a film. Maybe you can hear it.

Peter Lyon and myself done a radio script for the DuPont Company, on their program "Cavalcade of America," which won the ribbons for being their "most American Cavalcade," all built around a big long ballad I wrote about the "Life of Wild Bill Hickock," with a hundred-piece orchestra vamping an E chord in back of my guitar, and fully that many actors and stage hands hanging and running all over the place. The actors acted out each verse of the ballad after proper bridges and sounds by the orchestra and sound men. I can still hear the bullets and the ballad ricocheting off the sound box of my guitar.

Peter Lyon and me done this same thing later on for the CIO's program "Labor for Victory," with a smaller orchestra and another ballad called "The Girl in the Red, White and Blue." In this ballad, John Henry, Paul Bunyan, Driller Drake, Pecos Bill, and all of the champeen workers had a beer-drinking contest which was being toted to them by Polly Anne and the Girl in the Red, White and Blue. It was up on a big high mountaintop where they looked down on the world and seen the war coming on, and so the girls said, the man that does the most work to win this war will get all of the beer and all of the girls that he can rightfully handle. The men wheeled off to work, and the girls kept tabs on them from up on the sunny mountainside. The show and the song ended before the men got back, so the work was still going on all over the country. This program won loud clappings from the CIO and from the radio station, too.

I could tell you about other samples, but will try to keep close to what I am talking about. Oh, yes. We done this same thing over the barbs and wires of BBC, and won front-page reviews, pictures and all, in the leading British dailies, and then they made an album of records out of the show, with Will Geer, Burl Ives, Pete Seeger, Lee Hays, the Almanacs, and others, called "The Martins and The Coys." I think it was partly written by Alan and Elizabeth Lomax, and some others.

All of which brings me to what I am talking about.

Take some simple ballad, like "Goin' Down This Road" or "This Land is Made for You and Me," and follow the tracks of the singer from coast to coast. Commencing on the eastern seaboard, going down some one or several highways by number, and railroads by their names, stopping off to spend a night, an hour, a couple of days with every kind and color, every religious faith, every political brand and dye, every kind of seasonal work, every brand, mixture, and type of person that you would see on such a trip.

The ballad singer carries a pocket-sized tablet and an old penny pencil to scribble down a hymn, a blues, a good man and a bad man tale, a funny song, a doubletalk song, a talking blues, while he reads the words of his own songs slow and easy by lamp and lantern light, the lights of chandeliers, the lights of skies and weathers, by the lights of storms coming in, rolling away, the grayer lights of the flood basins, dust bowls, erosion centers, and all kinds of seeds in all kinds of grounds by all colors of hands. The same would go for all timber, oil, coal, ores, and up and down the skid rows across the streets from packing plants, the biggest factories, up and down the streets of the biggest industrial cities, and the littlest dots not big enough to be fly specks on maps.

The legal tender of the busking singer is songs, poems, spirituals, blues, shouts, chants, grunts, anything that can be written down to rhyme or time. He walks across political lines, color lines, conventional and superstitious lines, the lines of jealousy and blind hate, and even gets past the lines of the wildest drink, reaches a place in every person that no other sort of person can reach, and learns things about folks which no other sort of worker nor scientist can reach, not even the family doctor nor the priest nor preacher can reach, no, not even the union organizer, the sheriff, the deputy, the judge, clerk, the lawyer, school teacher, cop, nor anybody else.

He runs into stiffer points of conflict with all of them because every single one of them regards him as a competitor for the center of attraction, but we will show that all of these conflicts can be melted down in a short time. The feeling will be that the culture of the working people has always melted them together and drawn them into one when it was allowed to operate free as the wind.

He would travel by box car, by cushion, by ferry, by truck, by limousine, jalopy, by shoe leather, and would cross fields, orchards, rivers, mountains, swamps, and all of the uplands and the lowlands and the downlands. When by himself, the fight would be against the weather itself and against every kind of bug, animal, germ, and his own feelings of the lost kinds and the found kinds. Echoes of the songs and the music which he had heard would go with him through forests, deserts, and the million muddy creeks and rivers on a head rise. The chants and the cries of Indians signaling weather reports with drums, the wild sniffs, snorts, and stampedings of wild horses and cattle, could call up the old trail songs of the cowpoke and the little lost doggie.

He has got to learn a splattering of many lingoes, the Mexican, the Hungarian, the Italian, the Yiddish, the broad jokes of the racial kind which are almost the same in Sicily as they are in Indo-China. He has got to learn to thump a leatherskin drum, to play a juice harp and a harmonica, rattle the bones and the castinets, the strings of the saloon fiddle, the hillside fiddle, the banjo, the mandolin, and instruments of a hundred crazy kinds, all in order to get past the fences and quicksands of a thousand jealous suspicions. Everybody welcomes him, everybody suspects something devilish of him, and everybody gossips about him, and everybody breaks loose, everybody lets go, lets fly, and lets down their hair to the common thumping sound of his playing and the sandy scratching in his voice. He learns a million tricks of getting dimes in the taverns, and beds in the rich lodges, money for the poker tables, and his glass is never quite full,

never quite empty of the best homemade vino, beer, home brew, ale, cider, apple jack, gin, king corn, and imported bonded spirits. He rubs elbows with all classes, lives on all levels, speaks high philosophy or Bowery gossip in the same breath, clips the daily papers for stories about which to make up more songs and more ballads. He dances barefooted on the wet sands with the Louisiana field hands, and clogs with the Irishmen in a hard rock tunnel in Pennsylvania, dances with the half breeds and the full bloods of several Indian tribes, and knows the dead thumps on drums of all kinds, as well as most of their whoops and hollers. He drinks with their strongest thinkers and thinks like their hardest drinkers. He drinks several officials under their tables at banquets, picnics, rallies, affairs, dances, and the likes where he was singled out to be the brunt of some gag. He uses one and the same old hat of a muckledy dung color to collect all of his tips in everywhere he goes, and the hat is pictured and seen down on every kind of a floor you would see in these forty-eight states. He calls for letters which have been forwarded to him through seventeen states, and crams his writings into fat envelopes, shoe boxes, and small crates, to mail them back to somebody somewhere to keep for him. The songs are soaked with the sweat of several hands, and nearly faded out, when they are mailed home.

He sings his songs just for the fun of it at three or four little hometown radio stations, by himself, and then with others in studios, such as the ladies aids, the sisterhoods, brotherhoods, auxiliaries, the grand orders or everything, and parades with centennial marchers in a dozen places. He follows rodeos, carnivals, fairs, conventions, and the likes, and reads the *Billboard* magazine thin, in order to get to a certain spot ahead of time and fix him up a good place to play and sing. He spends his money like water sometimes, and some of it he sticks in an envelope to send to somebody. He sleeps in every kind of a bed you can think of, and down on every kind of a soil, under every sort of a tree, weed, bush, and in every kind of a hobo jungle camp.

He gets wet, dirty, frozen, blistered, and windburned, as well as hailstoned, lightninged on, snowed and rained and sleeted on, and is blown through six different colors of dust storms, cyclones, stiff winds and blue northers. He fights to keep his guitar covered from the weathers, and is sheltered by shantymen and mansion dwellers.

He is shown to partake of and then pass on over several good chances to dwell in worldly riches. He is welcomed into guarded estates, served from underground wine cellars as big as small towns, and fed from silvery trays of maids, butlers, and received by many doormen in heavy uniform. He is lectured to on the silliness of living such a footloose exist-ence when the doors of studios, stores, and fancy restaurants, etc., can be constantly opened to him. He does not say why he goes on, why he passes all of these things by, but the whole of the picture and story up to now would more than answer this in the minds of the onlookers. What is it that he has found that opens all of the doors to him, rolls the rugs out under his feet, and what is it that causes him to answer with a blank look, a sideward glance, with a bowed head, or with running, walking, or scrambling away from such offers like out from some sprung trap?

He is a mystery to everybody except to his own self. He is even lectured to by timberjacks, cowboys, foremen, good citizens, home renters and home owners, drug and prescrip-tion store owners, and by members of the left and right wings of the labor struggle. He sings around at strikes, on picket lines, or workers' meets, picnics, rallies and at big banquets with mayors, labor leaders, and government men and women, and the very next time you see him he is out walking along with his old penny pencil and his sweaty nickel tablet again. What heart of the people has he found, what passport, what ticket, what philosophy and what religious faith has he found that takes him on out to the roads and the trails of the organized and the unorganized again?

Of course, more expert scriptmen than I will have to hack and cut and paste all of this together. I am only writing what the ballad and the song and the busker would most likely come up against and through in such a coast to coast trip. His same old ballad would keep echoing back again to carry his mind and his feet on out and up and down some long, lonesome, moneyless road. The theme is that he cannot always tell nor make plain what a big and terrible spirit he has learned to live in. He is always paid back more than he puts in. His terrible lonesomeness at times is paid back by an equal amount of warmest welcoming. His days and nights in all kinds of weathers are paid back by a look that he sees and knows in the peoples' eyes and on their faces. This is his pay, his learning, his whole wealth, and his whole knowledge, this, and the millions of words that they all dig out of their deeper selves and swap to him for his gifts.

You can see here the thousands of good chances to bring in your flashbacks and pannings. Your mike and camera would be free to bring in all of the sounds and echoes of a whole people living in a world of work, sweat, tears, and rejoicings. The religious faiths could all be shown to vibrate with the same sounds and to reflect the same simple and honest dreams of a good world. You could flash their tearings down and their rebuildings, their lost seeds and the ones that took root and sprung. You could flash a whole race of people happy with a handful of clean leaves. You could flash the rhymes and beats of all kinds of works being done. Roads and buildings built, bridges and levees built, and timber dropped, snaked, dynamited and sawed up into shapes of houses. You could flash the big power dams, the light-metal factories, the plastic shapes of things to come.

I am writing you this because I've always wanted to do something like it. With your ear and eye and sense of vision-

ing, the parts I've left empty could be filled in. The actual
script would almost have to write its own self as we shot and
sang from place to place and as we climbed the several kinds
of back fences and opened the front gates.

I will stop now because I can smell Marjorie frying something in the kitchen and I've not had no breakfast yet. Besides we're going swimming and soak some vitafones up.

July 17, 1946

Seasay

All you seamen ought to be like me and make your home on
the lousy sea.

* * * *

My land needs fixing some and my land needs done up right.

* * * *

Where does the money of a seaman go? Out the bung and
down the hole.

* * * *

I gambled to lose down in Newport News
And the cop took me and the man turned the key
On the hard old lockup Rockwall jail
On that Rockwall hardup jail.

* * * *

It's only the factory owners that can broadcast how good
their things are and only the trade union that can tell
us how to get them.

* * * *

Most everybody I see knows the truth but they just don't
know that they know it.

* * * *

The only mistake that I made in this world was to walk the
dog with a dancing girl.

Slim

Tough Guy!

— Woody Guthrie —

Yes I am a seaman and I've seen this whole world
I sail on a rough stormy sea
And the only mistake that I made in this trip
Was to lose my money at cards man
And to lose my money at cards.

❋ ❋ ❋

I met her in the summer time
I kissed her in the fall
I covered her on cold winter nights
To listen to the pound of her heart and soul.

❋ ❋ ❋

That wave rolled in like a mountain man
And it left me here and thinking
About that night that I hit that port
And I lost my money drinking.

❋ ❋ ❋

What are all of them color strips there across your chest, sailor? Well, one is for Atlantic water. One is for Pacific water. One for Mediterranean water. One for sea water salt water fresh water dish water and good water bad water. My water your water river water and gutter water toilet water and rosewater.

❋ ❋ ❋

Do you know these waves have rolled off fifty million years and never lost a drop of water? No. All I want them to do is to roll me home without losing a drop of sweat.

❋ ❋ ❋

Dear Australia

Dear Australia:

By word of mouth I hear it said that you're about to come of age and that you're eying around for hotblood workers to help you turn some history pages, help you dress up in your prettiest, help you do some heavy sweating, help you throw your birthday party.

And, by that same word of mouth, east come west and north come south, by the jumpyleaf wiggly bark vine, by the winds blow, by the rains howls, by the screaming of the whirlpools, by the creaks and squeaks of hailstones, by the radio and papers, by the sun, the moon, and flood banks, by the fishy smell and riptide, by the barbed wire, by the whisper, by the hot hand, by the lamp lip, by the eye fires, and by runners, blowers, panters, and by God in Heaven, your coming of age is splashing around by word of breath.

I am just one little man speck in a packed and manspecked place, here. I'm not far from ocean's waters, I'm not far from chemical deserts. Not so far from mineral mountain. Not too far from slimey mine shaft. Just a speckle like a freckle on some face that's got too many. My elbow's not got room to move in. Nose ain't got no room to smell in. Eyes can't see no room to hope in. Ears can't hear no new plans walk down. And when I reach out with my jampackt finger, all I feel is lots more big herds, crowds, and swarms, and great big piles of these here buildings and these houses all raised up around my man specks. I'm in the padlock-shut door country. I'm in the pushy, shoving country, and the country that I'm caught in, rails and cusses for a footplace, heaves and hollers for some foot room, cries and squawls with fits of bawling on account of no more leg room. No more belly room. No more arm and shoulder spaces. No more hope and vision home-steads. No more free land nor no seed land, no more free-dom land to plant in.

This is just to give you a little bit of an idea of the place I'm in, and the tangleroot place my whole life's caught in.

My folks before me was what you might call goers, settlers, frontier-openers. I always feel my day's hot craving to tear off and be a hunter, and to run and be a finder, and a looker, and a liver and a sweater and a breather.

And my reddest hottest craving's always been to pull some sod up and to whip it into sunbrick, and to build my kids a house with. Or for my kids to build my house with.
I guess you're asking who I might be.
Wanting to know which place I from come.
Like to know which trail I tracked on.
Which bitterbite ranch I roped and tied on.
What stem of vines did my sap seep through?
Other things that you might ask me.
Other questions you might ask me.
I come from a place just about your same size.
My mama and papa looked just about like you.
My grandmaw's face had your same wrinkles.
Grandpaw walked just about like you walk.
And I guess I was born to run like you run, jump the way your kangaroos do, climb just as high as your wild vines there, splash up loud as your Bongo water falls.
And I was born in a windy high place, and I rolled off down a quicksand low place, jig danced in a swampy mud bog, burnt my hide on big hot sun rocks. Guess I got born just about like you did somewhere off down in a wiggletail water hole, and guess I crawled my way out of it and crept and stood my way up walking, found my hotair breath and talking, found my limber arm and leg dance, yelled my sidewinder whoop and holler, sung my play song, whistled my work tunes, sung my pay songs, hit my good dirt just like you did.
I done everything that you done.
'Course this was when I was just a kid run
Loose in the frontier Oklahoma sand hills.
Where I had so much free work room
That I stretched and growed in all nine windways,
I growed like you growed
'Mongst your wave sprays.
My dad he got borned in the sands of Texas down in a

boundary line called Bell County, under the shades of a short hair cotton stalk and in the shadows of a big slim castor bean. He come up to the Indian free lands called by the name of Oklahoma and he found my mama born there close to the smells of a bitter bark gypsum. Down off along a pecan bottom in some catfish drifts of the deep Fork River.

They had me and four more kids there in a little farmy ranch town up on a hill they named, Okemah.

All of us seen the farm and ranch town, over one night turn into an oil town. Jumped from a hay and a greencorn crossroad counting us, three hundred good souls, Indians, Negroes, whites, all equally scattered out there inside the city's limits. And we counted eyes and noses after the big oil field was dug down, when the riggers, and the drillermen, and the caser crew, and the pipers, and the canvas glove men got in, and after the roughneck, roustabout, ditch digger, tong bucker, team skinner, boiler maker, fireman, scouterman, lawyerman, talkerman, drinkerman, singerman, dancy lady, bayrum thinkers, extract guzzlers, canned heat squeezers, alky liars, fly by nighters, leaser man, royalty gal, and the new sheriff and the new law and the new judge and the new whore and the new pimp and the new ravers, fist fighters, card wheelers, slick fingers, and the holy roller yellers, and the non coms, and the snoose dippers, plug chawers, high riders, easy rollers, and after the mothers, fathers, and all of the oily others hit our town, like I told you.

We counted dead eyes and live eyes all over again and our little ranchy farm town had five thousand, five and a half, and then eight thousand, then we counted drunks and sobers and it run ten thousand over.

Crowds up and down the haybales
and the wagons and the buggies of our
place there

Running in and tearing around
scaring dogs, and scaring horses
till we had a crazy breakout and a
runaway every hour, and a house burnt
down every day there, and a gangfight
broke every night, and nobody'd even
stop to see a little old single fist
fight or a good fast walking cane
contest any more.
You got so many eyes, Australia,
I guess you seen where I went
When our third house it burnt down and my folks
all split and scattered. Some broke down and
lost their minds, some was hurt and took to
bed, some was off in places working, some
was rambling down some road shoulders.
Some along the Floodbank river. Some
took up to the Upper North Plain. Some
beat it out for a hotrock canyon, some
prospected the Rio Grande, some wheeled
out to the high Sierras, some crawled back
in a lead and zinc hole, some chased up a
big high jack pine, some tossed up some
big tall cities. I don't know where my
others went to. Some bummed off along
the Skiddy Row, some slopped up and
hit the Bowery, some said prayers in old
flop houses. Some made plays for short
job layers. Some got rich and some
got hungry, some growed fine and
some took sickly, some took down with
the chills and fevers. Some went down
the Sixty-Sixty, some went down the Ninety-Nine,
Some went down the Lincoln highway
Looking for work that's hard to find,

Looking for women lost out behind.

And I guess you seen me go all these crazy places.

Yes, I reckon, I do owe this globe here and the walkers on it a pretty big stack of stuff. And some that I tried to help the most, I don't know, but it looks like I sorta hurt them the most, oh, so they say. And so they wag a lip to tell. And these folks hate me like a snattlerake, like a hilly monster lizzard, like some horny desert bush rustler, like some coldblood crawling creeper. Like some long tooth oozy strangler. Like some wound-arounder choker, like some frothy-lipper mad dog.

If you'll say so,
And you'll let me,
I'll yell back acrost these oceans,
I'll bark back acrost your coral sea,
And in at their old windows,
And I'll josh and joke and tease them
And I'll rib and razz and goose them
And I'll make them jump up and chase me all the
way
Back over your way
And they'll 'mount up to such numbers as
did settle other wild spots,
and they'll chase me and they'll cuss me,
and they'll walk and look and trail me,
and they'll beat the weeds and trace me,
and they'll carry a torch on my tracks,
and they'll yell and sing and chase me,
and they'll
come in such big wild packs
That their feet will tramp your weeds down
And their hands will knock your vines down
And they'll almost tear your hills down,
But, you see,
They'll stop for water holes,

And they'll stop along to cook stuff,
And they'll toss up little doggy tents,
And they'll throw up little cook shacks,
And they'll build a little wind break,
And they'll put a little store up, then they'll buy and sell and
   swap things,
                    OHHH, like knives, and guns, and horses,
                         and they'll get to doing dances, and they'll
                                                            stray
                    off through your love trees, and they'll fall
                                                        down on
                    your grass here, and they'll keep on cussing me
                                                    out 'cause
                    they hate my guts so bad,
                         but they'll hug out in these weedy spots,
                              and they'll rub a nose and kiss some,
                                   and the very first thing you'll see here
                                                            will be
                    little houses all down along
                              and little streets in between two houses,
                                                        and they'll
go hook up mules and horses onto sarrys, buggys, wagons,
and they'll crank up little Tin Lizzies, and they'll rev up
airplane motors, and they'll oil and grease some fireball and
some cannon ball streamline trains, and they'll dot their trail
with new towns such as you ain't seen till now.
         I can give to you this promise.
         I can tell you this what's true.
         I can vow and swear I worked this trick, word for
word, and scheme for scheme, when I called the
Hebrew children out to build up Israel's desert, when
I called the Scots and Irishers up to raise up Britain's
windows, or when I called those two good Indians out
to help me dump them tea crates over and down and
into the waters of old Boston's seaspray waters. I got

people to the west coast to lift old 'Frisco up there on
her old steep uppy down hills, and we built L.A. this
same way.

Folks won't hate me any more, though,
When I trick them down your trail, there,
No,
    They'll all quit hating my guts
       and they'll all come stick their hand out
       for me to grab and shake
          while they tell me how glad they feel
       just because I
          pulled them by their tails half way around
the world
Here to the new come place, Australia,
Here where I been belonging all down along.
I crawled way back in all of them, I guess, trying to
look and see if I could see hit nor hair of some more of my
folks.

I kept my ear and my eye wide open to see all of my folks
crawl back in all of these old goofy crowded crazy holes and
places. I kept my mouth open and my ear to the sun and to
the wind, night and day winds, day and night suns, just letting my finger feel around to try to find some kind of a spot,
some kind of a hole, some kind of a work job, some kind of a
crawling place that would make just a little bit more sense
than all of these foney joints and screwball places my folks
are lost off and cornered up in right now.
So I guess
    I had as many good reasons to keep my eye on you,
    As you had to keep your eyes on me.
       Maybe you been sorta off out acrost yonder watch-
         ing me
       Just about like I been out over here watching you.
       We just didn't know that we was watching one
         another

Till it all got spread around by word of mouth.
Your name's Australia.
Australia's your name, I guess you know who I am.
Australia's a good name to slide around over
my tongue. Even tastes lairpin.
But you got lots of other names that dance around
in my heart just as pretty.
Names like Mittibiggi.
Names like Bongo.
Ever since they told me by word of mouth that
you are jerking your new gate open and singing for riders to
come and try you,
I been hearing names come tumbling
I been hearing names go rumbling
I been listening to pretty words whirling,
I been sprucing up going out girling.
Mittibiggi. Bongo.
Bongo. Bongo.
Mittibiggi Bongo,
Bongo Bonk.
Kiss that red lip.
Don't go too slow.
Bongo Bonk.
I come down to the Mittibiggi Bongo,
Mittibiggi Bongo, Bongo, Bonk.
Found somebody to hold my hando.
Mittibiggi Bongo. Bongo Bonk.
I hear old tales and dreams told in my newpage songs of
other years and other times. I hear a curious twist and a mix-
up of songs older than the human tongue, and newer than
our new moon rattling silver spoons
While the kangaroo beats his tail on a drum skin.
Drummy skin.
Leather skin.
Tummy skin drum.

And I'm an old hand when it comes to listening to the words from a tight leather drum. I hear signals of newer ages. I hear secret codes of factories jumping up. I hear the new kinds of yells and laughs, whoops and hollers, out of the eyes of newlycome settlers with a splotch of grass and flowers bubbling up and dribbling over every fence and every face. Open landers. Freeland finders. Frontier openers.

I'll not stop to read the want ads begging me to be polite when I ride nine trolleys down to scream back and forth at some filled-up office and a filled-up book and a filled-up ash tray, and a boss man that's all filled up with worry care of a million troubles. I'll go by this word of mouth news they're talking, by the way these folks are waking, by the way I see them striking out with new fires in their eyes. I'll go by the sound of the name, Australia, by the billibong, by the tucker bag, by the letters I see piling up asking you to let me in, let me in, let me come home, let me in. And, honey, don't flag your blind till I get with you on the warm side.

And if I can't find your dry side
And your good side and your warm side,
Honey, sugar,
I'll fight to ride the storm tide
  Just to be there on your bad side
  Just to touch you on your wild side,
  Just to touch you on your wild side,
  On your dusty windy rough side
  On your dusty windy rough side
    On your mean & onery sad side
    Till we pass the worst of riptides
    And you feel me at your cold side
    Till you turn to me
      Your sunny side.

There are just so many good wild times that we can have together, Australia,

That's why I do really hope out here in this pushy crowd, that you'll not lose sight of me in your night eyes,

We've both got lots of lost places somewhere here in us,
Places that nobody's not ever found so far till now.
I know how I feel here in my lost places, in my vacant
empty places, in my places that need finders and in my
places that need you to open them up.

I'll help you to find your own lost things in all of your own lost places. And you'll make me work in such new ways that I'll sing up a dance every day about some late streak that you helped me to find off down here in my own lone self.

My lone self. Can I say such words?
Here where all these gangs crowd 'round me,
Here where all these droves push past me?
Here where all these feet walk through me?

Well, I guess I do feel donesome, woozy, rattly, empty, lonesome. Out of a job my two hands itch for. Out of a job my blood can boil for. Out of a dream that I can dance towards. Out of a plan that I can ooze towards. Here in a spot where I just can't see any trick to wiggle my way out. Caught in a tramble net of old debts, stuck in a tar pit of blind worries, hung up a tree limb of hobbled down-payments, stuck off in a crowdy corner to spit in the faces of blood kin relatives, piled on top of my paw in law and here in the skirts of my maw in law, and mad and ruffed up at my brother in law, and hateful and mean at my sister in law, and crazy in my soul and my breast to feel grass grow, and going screwloose just to raise me some babies. God knows, Bongo Bongo, and the little green angels know, Mittibiggi, maybe you can feel out around you there and find me and my old itchy work hands some kind of a good job of work I can do,
And, yes,
I'll grow farms,
I'll plant towns,
I'll chop and weed hills for buildings that'll dance and sing up towards your skies there,

Sky houses, sky factories, up in your mist yonder,
Sky places, sky faces, sky windows hung full of all
colored face flowers
>   hoping new things
>   to the tunes of old waters
>   seeing new work done
>   >   by loud gangs of laffers
>   keep your eye on me, your hopes, too,
>   >   Australia,
>   Keep your lamp hot and just keep your globe
>   scoured,
>   Keep your steel oiled good,
>   And keep your broom sweeping,
>   >   Keep your fog rolling and keep your mist lifting,
>   >   Keep your duds on good, and keep your chin
>   >   upwards,
Keep your old nose clean, and keep your fish jumping, keep
>   your eye bright and keep your sheep nibbling,
>   >   Keep your lambs bleating and keep your calves
>   >   suckling, keep your grass growing and all
>   >   your winds blowing.
>   This is me listening here.
>   This is me walking.
>   >   This is me feeling along.
>   >   This is me coming.

I don't feel at home around this world here no more.
My house ain't here.
This ain't my settling down grounds.
I feel bossed and windy tossed, but, Bongo Bongo, I
>   sure ain't lost. This here is me coming.
Me out yonder listening to your own word of mouth going
all around this world. You're my word slinger. I'm your good
ear. I'm your listener. I'm your comer. I'm your down and
up traveler. Your outgoer. Your muddy splasher, and your

rocky stumbler. I'm your hunter and I'm your finder. You just
keep a lamp lit for me. You just keep a glass washed for me.
You just keep a door key for me.

You just keep a little place for me. And I'll take
and rest my new head in a pallet down on your floor.
I'll lay down
And dream out a new kind of a twist,
And I'll lay here and dream up some new kind of
a way,
New kind of a twist,
Some new kind of a way to do all of these little jobs I
got lined out here.

I'll wrastle you a river down and throw you a big dam over
acrost it that'll milk your cow, turn your wheel, light your
work up, light your eyes up, shoe your baby, crank your car,
start your diesel up, run your easy train, mail your letter, cash
your pay check, churn your butter, tan your hide, shake your
breast milk, fly your sky wagon, spray your paint brush, clean
your kitchen, cook your good meal, perk your coffee, juice
your lemon, kiss your sweetie, hug your sugar lump, and raise
up your new kids.
I'll show you quick tricks
What all you can do with your crops and
hides,
What all you can make out of stuff
you're wastin',
I'll write letters home to the folks I owe
money, I'll bring over a thousand, and bring
a blue jillion
work hands
that can mix more good cement and
plastic,
good stitchers, good knitters, old yarners, tall talers,
seam smellers, smart fellers, cog wheelers, machine lovers,

whistle listeners, chord strummers, tune fiddlers, and all
kinds of folks that work, love, and dance and sing just by
ear. My folks that I owe can trail me over here and then
when they get a little look at you, they'll all tell me I
don't owe them another lousy penny,
> And all just because,
>> I set down and wrote such free handed
> letters all back to my relatives
> they're all pioneer openers at their bottoms I guess.

You to Me

Then let this be
From you to me;
Let this be freed from words heard;
Let ours be heard in every heard word;
Let this between us two be said in every bed;
Let this that lays between us be spoke alone and only
> in our secret code word nobody else knows;
Let
Everything that moves between us
Stop its moving till there's not anything moving between the
> both of us;
How do you feel?
What do you think about it?
How does my word strike you?
I already know how I feel about it;
But I'm asking you now how you think and feel about it?
I sure don't like for so many kinds of things to always be
> happening and moving and taking place between us;
I don't like for any of these things to try to part us;
I never did like it when any of them got in between us and

stayed in between us for more than a few little snaps;
I wonder how we can
Fix it to where none of these crazy things
Move in between us anymore?
How can we fix things around to where not one little atom of
    a thing sticks nor stays between us?
I say for the two of us to come on and stay so close together
    that none of these moving things will have any room to
    ramble around between us;
I don't much like the looks of anything I see that circles in
    its circle here in between us;
I don't like to feel anything in between us;
Not one dang thing in between us;
All these ways and distances
And miles and trials and bottles and vials and
Hammers and files
From where I'm here at
To where you're now atting;
Betwixt and between us;
From me to you there;
Or from you over to me here;
From
You to me.

The Singing Cricket and Huddie Ledbetter

Just off-handed you might think that us human beings is
about the only outfits that can sing. Singing helps to keep you
going, it might not be all that keeps you going, but it's a
mighty powerful way of telling somebody that you aim to
keep going. He might think he's got you in a pretty hard

spot, but there's lots of ways out from between a rock and a hard place. Singing, if you hear it in a foreign language of some kind, is just so much noise; but you can listen to it a little bit, and you can tell just by the sound of it if you're supposed to go to making love, swaying your hips, or grab up a gun and go to marching.

Civilization is spread more by singing than anything else, because whole big bunches can sing a particular song where not every man can join in on the same conversation. A song ain't nothing but a conversation fixed up to where you can talk it over and over without getting tired of it. And it's this repeating the idea over and over that makes it take a hold. If the conversation is about good crops, or bad, good politics or bad, good news or bad, good anything else or bad, the best way to circulate it amongst the people is by way of singing it.

The politicians don't pay enough attention to singing. They pay attention to their own way of singing, but they don't listen to the songs of the people enough; for this reason they don't listen to the people enough, don't know what the people think, what the people want, what the people need, what the people do, where the people come from, where the people go, and what they are toughing out, and what they wish and hope for. For these reasons most politicians are plumb off track. They got a whole system of life and living, eating, drinking, celebrating, poker playing, exercise and athletic pastime, as well as book reading, going to meetings, shaking hands, etc., etc., figured out. That system of living and that way of doing things ain't no more like the people's way than nothing. When a young politician leaves his old home town and makes the trip to Washington he usually is a good example of the real thing, except that he draws his whole force and backing, he thinks, from the business folks in the town, at any rate it was the businessmen's money that got him the votes or fixed it to where he could run for the office—; but even their way of living ain't like the real old honest to goodness people that swing the last power in this old world; so if you leave your home country and go to the Capital City, you ought to watch awful careful to see where the song of your people goes and to go that direction with your vote.

I recollect an old black cricket that was about the best singer for his size that you ever seen. He'd sing and you'd hear it right real early of a morning. He'd sing while you laid there in bed and catnapped around, and dreamed that you got up and walked across the cold floor barefooted and built a big hot fire in the old wood stove, and he'd be singing right on when you woke up in about a minute or two and seen that you hadn't done a lick of fire building. This old cricket actually sung two thirds of the folks in that part of the neighborhood off to work. He'd sing if you had breakfast and he'd sing if you didn't.

Funny thing, I remember it was the mornings when I didn't have no breakfast that I had plenty of thinking time to set and listen to that old stickery-legged varmit sing. Nobody ever heard of a man talking to a cricket. I talked to this one. I use to mention him to my wife. "Listen to that son of a bitch sing, wouldn't you." Once in a while she'd mention him, "I don't see how he sings so loud, do you?"

He sung so loud that the neighbors could hear him when they drove up outside. They'd say they heard the same kind of singing over at their house. I guess these here crickets had framed up to sing in all of the houses. I remember old lady Hill said once, "That's about the best singin' I ever hear any more, since Joey had to sell his banjo; he couldn't keep no strings on a banjo nohow, cost a dime ever time you bust one, an he's always six mile from town when one flies a loose."

There's an old damp saloon over the ridge here at one of them little stops that's about to rot down at the foundation, and the old bar man has been right in there all of his life, and he's getting awful old and grouchy for the past several years. He's got an old cricket over there, too, just about the same caliber as this one I'm talking about, and that old cricket gets up in under the drip there somewhere and dens up and sings his daylights out. He's raised a couple or three families back up in under there. One of his families is twice as big as yours, so that makes it, you would have to live two lifetimes to make up for his one, less'n you got a awful big family hid out somewheres. This old bartender don't like no nickel singing machines in his place. All he's got is just that old cricket over there, but his business is better than them neon saloons down in Johnsonville. He's got one right young boy that rides in there from about eleven miles back north and a little west, and he comes over there to set and listen to that cricket. That's one reason. It's closer over to Johnsonville than it is to this old joint, but he drunk three bottles of strong beer one night and said he didn't like them neon lights 'cause it shines in the girls' faces and made them look like they was dead corpses.

The main secret about singing ain't so much to have other folks listen to as it is to pick up your own spirits. This old cricket used to sing on the railroad, under the ties, and he'd be up and out a singing about three quarters of a hour before the hands come down to work. I use to be a coming in home after a blow somewhere along towards sunup, and when I'd make the crossing right there at the main road, I'd ride down the railroad track and cut across the back pasture home; and it would be before the section hands got on the job and you'd hear that old cricket over there a letting her out. He just must of sung for his own good more'n anything else.

The best and loudest singer that I ever run onto his name was Huddie Ledbetter and we all called him Leadbelly, his arms was like big stove pipes, and his face was powerful and he picked the twelve-string guitar. He told me once down at his house, "I sing early of a mornin' 'cause it picks me up an' I cain't make it good to you 'less it's good to me . . ."

That old cricket must of felt that same way. He'd warm up for his own good for a good long spell and then when it got real good to him, it just naturally got good to you. You cain't make nobody like your singing if you don't like it yourself. If you don't feel good over it, neither will anybody else. If I'm singing in a red light saloon and I find out that my singing's a getting flat or to where I don't like it, I always get up and walk out, 'cause I wouldn't take a penny's tip for singing a song I didn't like.

You just cain't fool nobody with your singing no matter how much money you're a getting paid for it.

When it comes time for people to actually get up and go to marching, if you've been a putting on with your singing, they'll most of them up and march the other direction.

Crickets sing in under chunks of old rotten wood, like houses that ain't painted and barns that's coming down, and farm houses that's been up and deserted, and old wired-up furniture, and in old stuffy apartment houses where the wall-boards is loose and falling down, and the floors are all soaked with spilled lard and the stair steps are creaky and liable to throw you down. Barns and toilets and old swayback farm buildings is a good place. Anywhere there's anything rotten. This is because, you might not believe, but this is a warm place. This is good fertilizer for this kind of singing. Erosion, mold, rot, decay, damp, crooked work, lies, broke promises, profit snatching, you will hear him singing around all of this. And when you lift up your head and cock your ear back to listen, you'll look up—and you'll just stand there a looking away out across yonder, a listening just like everybody else does.

Somehow or another the best singing just naturally comes from under the leakingest roof.

You know why folks like to hear a cricket sing? You might

not be able to see just exactly why it is, or what good a dern little old cricket does. Well, it's like this, when you hear a cricket you can just look around a little and find a rotten board and plank that needs to be jacked up and a new one run under it.

Politician guys that hatch out through these here paper and pencil colleges and drug store school houses are pretty well agreed that there ain't much work that needs to be done, or if they can sing together long enough to decide that there is, they get off key on how it needs to be done. They cain't stay together on their song. They cain't keep their mind off from their pocketbook long enough. One feller off of the good chord can screw up the whole singing. They say they don't see no work to be done, ain't no jobs a building stuff up. But the little cricket he says there's plenty of rotten stuff that needs a fixing.

> Tear down the rotten stuff;
> Put up new;
> Clean out the rotten plank;
> Put up a new;
> Tear out the rotten floor;
> Lay in a new;
> Get off of the rotten side;
> Get on the new.

Crickets don't eat houses down. Crickets just hang around to sing that the damn thing's a falling down. He'll be there a long time singing about it. You get to where every time you see a cricket you think of the house about to fall down. But he didn't bring it down. Then the other bugs that really brought the house down will run off somewhere and they'll say, Look at that god damn cricket, he was there all of th' time! He's th' one! Get 'im! He lives in rot an' filth all of th' time! He causes it! He believes in it! He spreads it around! Get that bastardly son of a bitch! And the cricket don't want to live nowheres else. He had to stay on the job and holler and sing that the house was rotting down. He had to stay. He couldn't sing nowheres else. There wasn't nothing to sing about nowheres else. So he stuck. He got blamed for all of the rotten work. But he stayed.

Finally one day over in the wood box behind the stove, or down in the barn by the manure pile in the sun—somebody thought that he was mean and hurting them, and squashed him under a shoe sole. But his relatives heard about it, and they sing about it. His brothers and his sisters heard about it and they sing about it. They stay around old rotten barns and houses and sing about it.

They sing the song called, The Song of the Singing Cricket.

February 2, 1941

Abuse

I've abused in my ignorance every good thing I saw grow up around me.

I abused every good idea with a hail storm of low thoughts.

Every kindhearted friend I've hurt, insulted, belittled, and bruised badly.

I abused my own body every way I could do it, but somehow, my body stays in perfect health.

I've walked half days and whole nights to say a hasty, mean, and ornery word to not only my first and finest friend, but to my own wife as well.

I've abused her most of all, and she has been the only thing that made my world make sense.

Abuse

Is the one word which I really have made full use of.

I wore it plumb out.

Jack Elliott drew me
thiesa way and I
sure do hope I
look this good.

Woody Guthrie

Abusing

I don't care how you use or abuse my name.
Woody Guthrie is a genie to everybody but his own self.
I abuse him lots worse than you do, or you ever will.

I don't care what you say about what I do, because I know
    that
You caused me to be or to do whatever I am or have done.

I don't care
What you say about me
Just so you say it.

> *April 13, 1948*
> 3520 Mermaid Avenue
> Brooklyn 24, N.Y.

Dance a Little Longer

Eats an' drinks an' smokes are gone,
Ice on th' steps an' you cain't git home;
Hang y'r things on th' peg in th' corner;
Giggle an' wiggle an' dance a little longer.

Chorus: Dance aroun', dance a little longer,
           Just gotta hold you justa little longer.
           Sing an' talk, joke a little longer;
           Just gotta hold you justa little longer.

Rained three days an' th' barditch full,
I cain't git home, it's a muddy old pull;

woody Guthrie

I live on toppa that bad hill yonder
That's why I gotta dance a little longer.

(Chorus)

Tonight's th' night that th' muddy flood come,
Took my house and it tooken my barn;
Drowned my goose an' drowned my gander,
That's why I gotta dance a little longer.

(Chorus)

Lightnin' set my place onna fire,
Thunder shook down my floorin' boards;
Wild wind come along and it stole my lumber;
That's why I gotta dance a little longer.

(Chorus)

I tied my ship to a downtock dock,
Tidal wave run in an' give it a knock;
It wrecked my boat an' shivvered my timbers;
That's why I gotta dance a little longer.

(Chorus)

I tied my bicycle up to a post,
An' it got stole by a graveyard ghost;
He won't bring it back till you kiss me stronger;
That's why I gotta dance a little longer.

(Chorus)

I hadda date tonight witha gal down th' road,
Told 'er I'd stop off an' dump my load;
She's pretty pretty, but you're lots perttyooee;
That's why I gotta dance a little longer.

(Chorus)

Since I got a whoof of th' way you smell
Alla them other gals can jump in th' well;

She smells strong, but you smell stronger,
That's why I gotta dance a little longer.

(Chorus)

January 27, 1950
3520 Mermaid Avenue
Brooklyn 24, New York

Singing Troopship

BROOKLYN, N.Y.
August 30, 1944

DAILY WORKER WORKERS AND READERS
(May your herd increase):

Well, I had to sail out and get hit again for the second time. It looks like I am just naturally born to stop high explosives. I was at Cherbourg just after D-Day, and they hooked some tugs onto us and took us back to England where I saw a lot of Hitler's flying bombs in action. I saw thirteen come low over our ship and explode not too far away. They make a goofy sound and a hell of a big explosion, and they hurt women, and kids, and innocent folks of all kinds. Yes, the only way to stop them is to send in every single man we've got, and blow those rocket bomb bases fifty-nine miles right straight up.

I was brought back on a troopship and we had a good NMU crew, even if the captain wasn't so union-minded. We wrote 1,034 letters to Congressmen, on the three bills: 1) GI Bill of Rights for Seamen. 2) Citizenship for Alien Seamen. 3) Unemployment Insurance for Seamen. These are all good bills and badly needed to make good laws. Most of the Congressmen answer by mail and make nice promises. (What's the latest market price on promises, good fat juicy ones, anybody know?)

We sung songs to the troops going over and as they unloaded into their invasion barges. Your backbone tingles like public-owned electricity when you hear five or six hundred good, lonesome, hard-fighting soldiers and seamen get to singing these Union War Songs together. It means that the history of the world is reflected right here in these oily old waters under you, and as their voices tremble against the steel and out across the waves, you are just about the gladdest person in the whole big world, somehow or another.

Jimmy Longhi, Cisco Houston, and myself had a sort of a NMU Trio, sort of a Torpedoed Seamen's Outfit. The soldiers, lots of them, hadn't ever sang any such Union Songs, and they didn't know that a song could say anything about anything. I will always believe that these soldiers are Union Men at heart. They rave and chant, and whoop and roar and they holler, "Hey! Hey! Bring them Union Boys back! Th' Union Boys! Union Boys! Bring 'em back! Back! Back!"

This goes on and on when you stop the music and the singing. We go back to our own quarters or to our messroom up above to shoot the gas over some coffee, and the men down below are actually rocking the whole convoy with their yelling, "We want th' Union Men! Union Men! Union Men! We want th' Union Men! Union Men! Union Men!"

And so, of course, we look at each other, and tighten our bellies up a few notches and pray that our backbones will hold out for another hour or two session of lung busting and Union Singing.

We found men from down south, out west, everywhere, good musicians, and we lent them our mandolins, fiddles, guitars, and taught them these new Union Words to the old tunes that they had already been playing all of their lives. I've never seen any such dancing and high prancing. I have never seen a square dance that will stack up beside the ones

that these troops pull off, holding hands, swinging pardners, skipping through the salty dew.

Somehow, I don't know, but somehow, it seems like you get to thinking about everything both good and bad that you've done in your whole life, and you sort of let it all gather up inside your system, and you see that you are out there risking your life, and you just want to lay your head back and wiggle your ears and sing so loud and so long that all of the good and the bad will sort of mix up and boil around and come out of you. You feel that way. Every man does. He wants to get his whole life's history, worries, cares, troubles, hopes, hurts, fears, debts, everything, all off of his chest all at the same big blow. And here on the ocean with seven other oceans on each side of you, is the perfect place, and so when you hear a song that the whole bunch is singing and that song tells just exactly what you've been thinking all the way from boot camp to here—well—I can't tell you—I can only sort of hint at the whole picture. These men here. These Union Soldiers hearing their song.

Oh, how I'd love to see a couple or three hundred moving pictures that could just half way hit this same spirit and this same truth in their flickerings. Men of all colors, all tongues, all states, out here on this big ship, finding their own selves, and finding their own words, their own minds, their own feelings, thoughts, plans, and their own Union (many, many, for their first earthly time).

We can't begin to thank the National Maritime Union enough for the good work in this direction. While men are aboard ships, and while they are ashore, the NMU gives them this same working spirit. The NMU gives lots of us our first toehold, and teaches us how to speak out, to stand up and how to use our mind, how to be a man. How to do all kinds of political action work. How to step lively. How to sing. How to sing in your soul.

One funny thing, while I'm thinking about it, and about movies.

When this ship got hit (I'm not allowed to say how), anyway, several boys were down in the troop messhall seeing a movie, *White Cargo*, with Hedy Lamar.

The explosion throwed them up into the air and bounced them all around in the dark—just at the very moment when Hedy was being led out into the tall timbers by some man. The love scene was getting hot. Weeds. Bushes. The smell of the earth and of Hedy. Birds. Shadows from old ignorant trees. Hedy. The man. They kissed, and it lasted for several running feet of film. And then, it was *Keeeebbbbloooommmm!* And the men went up to the ceiling, back to the floor, up again, back down again, and many of them were cut and bruised somewhat, although they didn't know how bad right this moment.

They made a high dive for the picture machine, grabbed the rolls of film out (it was all wrecked), and fought like tigers for the scraps of film. I had already grabbed my guitar and lit up the stairs and was on the main deck waiting to go over the side in a lifeboat. It was foggy and damp and bad. I stood there plunking and listening and wondering where in the devil all of them were at. Jimmy and Cisco were there with their mandolins and fiddles, and we all wondered if the whole crew had been hurt. (The soldiers had already gone ashore in their invasion barges a few hours ago.)

In a few moments, out rushed the crew who had been to the movies. Their gear was mostly just the little square hunks of the film which they had snatched in the movie below.

They burned up most of the electricity in our rescue lamps trying to hold the little scraps of film up to the bulbs to see what happened to Hedy and the man out yonder in the trees. They hung onto those hunks and bits of film like Hoover onto a dime.

We gathered around and sang some more Union Songs

WHAT DOES
THE BOOK SAY
ABOUT
HIGH
ALTITUDE?

waiting there in the fog for the tugboats to hook onto us and pull us back into Cherbourg. We waited here overnight and then they tugged us across the English Channel back to some port in the south of England. And this is where we lay as we watched our whole fleet fire away at the Nazis' rocket bombs.

Thirteen. Thirteen the very first night. Millions of red streaks in the sky overhead where the bullets chased after the bombs. Some of them were brought down. Others went on, ran out of gas, ducked down, and then exploded with a big boom and a loud jar.

On my way back I had plenty of time to make up some new songs. I made up more than thirty, which I'll record for the Asch Record people. I'm not too positive when they'll be released, but I'd like for those soldiers, and lots and lots of other soldiers everywhere, to hear these Union War Songs on their radios and loudspeakers. (Big Money don't like for one single word that makes sense to come over those radio speakers. But maybe in the Union World, I'm positive that's what we'll all be hearing, Union Songs about the Union Man fighting for his Union World. And Big Money can just take its old sissy, phoney crap, and dump all of it over into the ocean, like we done with the Boston Tea!)

I read Earl Browder's book *Teheran* on the ship coming back.

I believe this is the best book that I've read so far about the whole globe, the whole orange, this whole big egg that we're living on. I've already knocked off more than a dozen songs about the ideas that flew through my brain as I read Mr. Browder's book. Union Spirituals. Union Blues. Union Ballads. Union Rags, Polkas, Fox Trots, and Two Steps. Union Everything.

In my own brain, my own mind, I have given Thomas Dewey such a stiff beating, that I doubt if I could write it down here on paper. I spent ten years thinking up reasons why I didn't like Herbert Hoover, and now I multiply that by nine and I've got Dewey. I'm one guy that's stuck my head in many a Hooversville and many a garbage dump, jungle camp, shacktown, and have seen more of this than I ever hope to stomach.

But, since all of the Fascist-lovers and Nazi-lovers sent Dewey valentines on his day of nomination, all of the whole Fascist breed and stripe are on one big hunger wagon now, and it's mighty easy to see it. It's easy to spot them and to know them. They are all on one big train. In one big Fascist smelling camp.

And so, the picture is plainer now. The enemy is out there in plain sight. The Union Workers and Voters drove them out of their ten thousand little hiding holes, and forced them, herded them, coralled them, all over into one BIG Republican Camp.

I think this is really something to sing about.

I think all of our ships are singing about it. All of our farms and factories are humming and yelling about it. All of our mines echoing it. Our big trees whispering it. Our waters are babbling it.

All of you Fascists are over now in one big rat hole.

Enclosing a song called the "Ballad of Teheran." I'd like to dedicate it to Earl Browder, to his wife, Raisa, and to Joe Stalin, Winston Churchill, and to Franklin D. Roosevelt. And to every drop of Union blood in all the Union veins around the world tonight.

WOODY GUTHRIE

My Secret

Nothing in this earth life is vulgar to me.
Nothing around this planet's crust is lowdown to me.

I see nothing obscene around me no matter where my ten senses go to scratch around.

I can't see one thing indecent about any of the cells nor germs, nor plants, nor bugs, nor insects, nor skybirds, nor seeds of man.

To call God's highest works (man) by some sort of a fearful obscene name would in my set of books be the worst of sins.

Man's clothes and man's drapings have not one snap to do with making him any more noble, any more honest, any more upright, nor any more wiser than he is when he puts on another few dollars' worth of draperies or when he sheds them all and cometh forth wearing no more than his naked skin.

There is no known article of duddery, wrappery, bandagery nor of clothing which is one one thousandth as pretty, as free, as healthy, and as miraculous as the naked skin of even the worst, ugliest, dirtiest, sickest, human being on the face of this earth.

Lots of good fine people here and yonder have oftimes accused me of being more or less aware of some kind of a key secret which I use to go unlock all the gates and hard barred doors to get at every hideout holler of the human mind.

I've read a big mountain of books both good and bad on the subject of the soul, the heart, the spirit, the mind of man, but I've not stumbled in my labors so far upon any one medicine (that has not already been discovered and fairly well named and branded before I got to be born).

Love is the only medicine that I believe in. It enters into all other forms of good medicine and good nursing. To me the easy rub and gentle touch of the nursing hand is more potent and longer lasting in its healing powers than all or any other known drug medicine.

Love is the only God that I'll ever believe in.

The books of the Holy Bible never say but one time just exactly what God is, and in those three little words it pours out a hundred million college educations: and says, God Is Love.

And that is the only real definite answer to ten thousand wild queries and questions that I myownself tossed at my Bible. I mean to say, that is the only really sensible, easy, honest, warm, plain, quick, and clear answer I found—when I was ready to throw so-called fearful cowardly thieving poisoning religion out my back door, it was those three words that made not only religion, but also several other sorts of superstitious fears and hatreds in me meet one very quick death.

God Is Love.

God is really Love.

Love can be and sure enough is moving in all things, in all places, in all forms of life at the same snap of your finger.

Love is the power of magnetic powers and repulsions that causes all shapes and forms of life to run to a hotspot and meet its mate.

Love works this wonder then in fifty thousand billions of uncounted trillions of life's forms, shapes, patterns, in every step and in every stage of life, in the lives of the living cells; in the lives of the living bugs; the lives of the living insects; the lives of the living reptiles; the lives of the living animals; and in the very lifeblood of all the living forms of birds; and in the same plain ways all through the moves and the actions, the very thoughts of every human being that travels here in plain view of our eyes.

Love moves them all.

And in all of them love does move.

And wherever I look to see a wiggle or a waggle or a shape of humanly form there I know is a thing not to be in any way hated, nor in any manner despised nor even feared, nor shadowed around with insane cold suspicions; but to test forever and for all my days and for all my nights, too, my powers of love, (I mean by that) my own powers to love.

Love casts out hate.

Love gets rid of all fears.

Loves washes all clean.

Love forgives all debts.

Love forgets all mistakes.

Love overcomes all errors and excuses and pardons and understands the key reasons why the mistake, the error, the stumble, the sprawl, the fall, was made.

Love heals all.

Love operates faster and surer than space or time, or both.

Love does not command you, order you, dictate to you, nor even try to boss your acts and your actions; love much rather asks for you to tell its forces what to do and where to go and how to build up your planet here by the blueprint plane of your warmest heart's desire.

Love can't operate in your behalf as long as your own sickly fear will not permit love to operate in your behalf.

Love is universal.

Love governs the spin and the whirl of this earthly planet all around through your skies here.

Love moves and love balances every other planet star you see there above you by the uncounted blue jillions.

Love moves and balances fifty billion and more kinds of powers and rays and forces inside every little grain of sand. And love causes peace and harmony to whirl a new whole universe on the inside of every little atom.

Love catches up with space.

Love outruns time.

Love makes the big world little and the little world big.

Love makes all good seed fertile.

Love multiplies and love divides.

Love is in the triggery works of all mathematical numberings.

Love moves to drive the weather and all of the powers of your elements. I see above all how your winds and your storms and all of your clear sunny skies are not just big accidents.

Love allows no accident to happen.

Love lets no waste occur.

Love wastes no ounce of motion.

Love works all mysteries.

Love works all miracles; yet I call no working of love a miracle. (Nor a mystery.)

Love labors only for the next good and welfare of the most people; for, by doing the most good for the most people, love operates fastest.

If it were not for that sun you see size up yonder in your sky every day, there could be no form of life take place on our planet earth; but the sun's rays are not your deathly enemy as faithless ones taught you to believe; that sun yonder I say to you is your very best friend if you take all its rays and give them a job in love to do. Love balances, holds, and controls all the moves and acts of the sun; the sun must shine by the grace and permit and by the very permission of love itself.

Love fires and burns and boils around in every inch of the great fiery belly and great fiery face of the sun, but love also does the same job for several other millions of great suns greater in size and power than yonder's daily new morning sun.

Love is all force.

Love is all power.

Love is all energy.

Love is all strength.

Love is all health.

Love is all beauty.

Love is all good work well done.

Love is all fun.

Love is all pleasure, all joys known.

Love is all eternity.

Love is here now.

Love is the thinker of every good useful thought.

Love is all there be.

Love is all space. There be no space that is empty of love.

Love ties all things together.

Love makes all things one thing.

Love lends all. Love takes all. Love flows over more with lovelights than all of the great splashes of all our great sunshiney waterfalls.

Love kisses above and down below your waterfalls.

Love makes all your good and bad laws and love takes up your own sickly laws and breaks them into sand grains just for the laffs and for the kicks.

Love is always glad to make you gladder.

Love feels sad when it makes you sadder.

Love works best when you give it a big job of work to do.

Love loves you most when you love love the most.

Love sees you best when you see love the best.

Love finds you when you find love.

Love finds you where you find love.

Love meets you where you meet love.

Love gives to you what you give to love.

Love loves most of all to work for you.

Love loves most of all to build up or to tear down as you desire and as you command.

Love forgave you all of your humanly sins back there twenty-six months before you ever came out of the womb of your mama's belly. You are already a good clean commander of all the forces and powers which love controls.

I say to you, take up your post and your command of love.

I say to you, take up your very own gift and talent.

I say to you, take up your power of command.

I say to you (and to all of you and yours), take up your word, the word of your command.

I say to you, this power to command the absolutely neutral

powers of love, this command is your very own birthright; no piece nor coin, no pile of gold, no penny paid, no dollar mailed, no stamp licked; no priest asked, no minister called —unless you so desire it and so command things to be thusly. (For the well and goodfare of most of us.)

Command love to work with you and for you.

Command love to operate in you and through you to heal, to help, to lift, to bless, to cleanse and to spread the good word and the good news that the day of human hate and fear and dark lostness is all over and all gone and a day of new bright command at your hand.

For your own sense of your own commandery will grow only as quick and as easy fast as you pass the great command (word) onto all of your dear dearly beloveds in humanly shapes of misery till your command sets them free unto their own commandery.

Tell your comrade, Comrade, bend down in dank fear traps not one second longer—Comrade—your love commands every known (and every unknown) kind of universal energy in existence, and that which has lain in the sad unknown for so many insane centuries, on this one day, by my one newfound word of command—is the insanity all choked out.

To love is to shape, to plan, to order and to command.

To know how to love fully you must learn how to command fully.

No human is full grown till the love tells him to command all. Fear before none. Quiver before nothing. Kneel at no spot. Beg no cure. Be a slave to none and master to none.

Command the skill.

Command the planets.

Command the starlights.

Command the very heavens.

Command love to move and to act for you and your sweet

mate—and for all the other such love pairs like you and your mate and your children.

Command your plan (in love) to come to pass.

Command your desire to happen.

Command and say:

"I command that all the powers and all the forces of love in my universe shine and make warm and friendly the labors and the seeds of man. I command that today's battle be badly lost to that soldier who is this day the greatest distance away from his home. I command all the rays of my good sunny shine to tear down my old city of hate and to build up my new towns of love. Destroy this day every law against love."

You, of course, know that my own command here is but my own sample for you to see to use to shape your own commands by.

The resolution in my union hall is a command passed on in love for the best welfare of the union members.

I just hope that you will now be a bit more hotly and keenly aware of your power as a love commander.

You have to learn to love even your most deadly bitter enemy if you'd rally but the most high peak trail of your own powers as a love commander. You must bring death to none and life to all or you'll just never quite tip the high top as a love commander.

Your love command must forever be just exactly the direct opposite of war's crazy baseless hatreds. Peace, peace and sweet, sweet peace must be the song of thy tongue tip. Peace is love. Love is peace. Your love command must for all eternity be your peace command.

Your every command must make your whole a better one to work in and to love on.

This whole crust of a planet is a pretty place to walk around over; I have not overlooked very many spots in my own walkings; but what we need around this world is a generation of bossy commanders in love in the place of our crop of scaredykat slaves friend in the oils of their own dreamy hate.

Hate can never command.

Hate can never be the boss.

Hate can't ever ever win an inch.

Hate can't stay. If you flush your own life down the floody drains of hate nobody weeps when you sink.

Hate has taken away whole crazy nations on top of nations.

Hate never took one single lover away.

One true love commander can turn the universes of hate into heavenroads and byways of love, love, love.

Sweet love.

Sweet love.

Sweet love.

Oh, poor poor sickenly soul of lost gambles, why why why must you rage and shake and beller and howl when you dent no heads but the one tied onto your rotten shoulders?

Why rage?

Why bellow?

Why shout and spit crazy in the wind? Why look blind?

You can't ever win.

You can't fight, because you can't see.

You can't see because you are so blind.

You are just blind on account of your own sick fears and your hatreds.

And you know all of this a good bit plainer than most any other human around you;

A slave to hate,

That is what you are;

A slave to your own hate;

That is all on earth you are now.

A crazy slave to crazy fear and crazy hate.

No more than a slave to your crazy dream that fever flashes

on your own picture screen; where you know most plainly that your hate and your own fear has chained you down for another one of its crazy howling weeping crying wailing and cursing slaves with all your sense of control gone, all your self-control, (your self-command,) gone out of you.

Love for these people all around you here can pick up your dying carcass and heal it up again as good as a new one.

Love is the only thing that can help you now.

Love is your only ray of good sunshine.

Love will give you back your self-control.

And love will put your own command in the palms of your hands.

And for you of the deathly dope drug, you of the crazy needle, the pill, the reefer fag, the hot spoon, the opee pipe, the dead mattress, the gone spirit, the gone life, the heavy headache, the crackling temples, the walleyed eyeballs, the spitty lips, the loud yells of choking sickness; the gun, the gat, the stickup, the fight, the cops, the big chase for more dope and for more guns and more stickups; your own fears and hates can be cured and healed up by one kind of love tonic, and one kind alone. Love will take your hand and lead you back to a job in my open sunlights.

Absolute slave you are today to your hateful despisable dopes, yet you can too step out here in line of the duty of love and take up a command post as sure and as certain as can any of the rest of us.

Space and time you shall command them both.

All things that be in time's own space you command all these along with the others.

All that grows in space's own time you too command and order these unto your heart's plan.

Your own heart will plant its plans for the great freed goodness of all my seeds of man;

And all my seeds of man will love to work and to build and to feed and to breed according not to webby old law books, but by the very law plan of the only soul and spirit.

And my body shall be my only soul and my only spirit;

And my spirit shall be only soul and body.

I command thus and so.

I have uncovered here one great good useful lesson to be learned by both armies now doing such loud marchings, the going capitalist, and the coming communist.

I can greet you on both sides and tell you now in plainer ways about your newfound love command.

We must rise up today from olden kinds of slaves to command the newly seen forces of nature. I sing a Ma and Pa Nature a lot closer to home.

That's all my new Bible book is: a command of nature and a control over all the forces of Ma and Pa Nature.

I'm Not the Man

I'm not the man that found more than you found.

I think today that you found lots more than I've run onto.

Or, on a second thought, would say, I guess we've both found the same amount.

I could say that the reason I make so much noise about the things I have found, is because I've found less than your eyes and hands have found.

You make just as much noise as I make.

You find something every minute and you make a big to do about it. You speak and talk and wave your hands around about a new thing you find or an old thing you dig out.

You speak and talk it out with your friends and with your neighbors,

And I write these same things down here with my stood-up words. The picture that you paint with your common and everyday words is much better to me than anything I'll ever write down, because I say that your spoken word is lots and lots better than my written word. I try to catch your feelings and your thoughts and ideas, but you throw my feelings out and up and all around, and I think your voice around your job, your bench, sink, stove, table, and bed is much better spoken than any feelings I will ever write.

This is the main reason why you mustn't think you can come to a book of mine and learn as much from me as I learn from you. No, you do not pause nor take the time to write your words down onto a typed nor a scribbled page. Your words have that beat and time, that rhythm and that breath of life which my written words do not and never can have. This is the reason why you must never think that the poet on the page can be as great as you in your own natural self.

You hear these seven birds up in a tree the same and as plain as I hear them. You talk about them and you make several people around you feel better when they hear your words rolling out from your lips and throat so alive and so warm.

And when I write down my words about the seven farmers and their juicy sweet daughters, you must know and feel that I am like an artist that draws you a picture, and the brush cannot ever catch the colors and the living feelings that your licking tongue can catch and speak. The written page is great and has always been great, but has never been so great to me as those words you howl, yell, laugh, recite, and sing a thousand times a day. For, if I could just get one short thought of your words actually set down with every live breath that you talk and speak them to your friends and to your family, well, this world would call me its greatest living and dying artist.

It is you, you see, not me only, but more you than me, that this world is hungry to hear about and to find. I am not trying to catch my own beats and my own rhythms as much as I'm trying to catch the roll and the sway, and the up and down movements and motions of your common wasted words that you toss off into your winds more certain and sure than the petals of any flower from any limb or stem. You are so full of new life seeds that you spray the winds with your words. I catch one or two of your deeper words here and there but you catch more words about me than I catch about you, and the way you say your thoughts is deeper and finer, greater in every respect than anything my line has ever snagged and landed. Keep up your plain gossip talking and your flat-footed tale telling, your mimicking, your imitating, your glancing, your hypnotizing and your suggesting, your operations of powers and gifts of your own mind and tongue. I will listen to you and try to catch in my own lifetime, oh, maybe two, maybe three, of your plain outspoken words, and I'll go down in history like the farmer that tried, like the sailor that made a stab at the ocean, like the factory hand that took a whack at it, like anybody else that tries to do any little job their hand and brain has set itself to.

I just wanted you to know this morning that it is you who inspires me more than I will ever inspire you. I come to your pillow and door for my inspiration. You'll not find in my book what I see in your face and hear in your voice. This is the whole truth, the honest truth and nothing but the truth so help us, God.

February 8, 1947
Coney Island

All of the Country

All of the country that I've seen
I always did like to call mine
And even while I was walking through it
Or riding past it looking at it
I always did like to call it mine
I first remember the scrub oak sand hills
Back down across Oklahoma
And all of the sticker weeds and grasses
That we got down in there
And the little gardens we grow
And then I next remember following
These same little sand hills
And deep rutty roads all the way down
To where the country gets flat
And the gardens get a little bigger
And the trees get to be pine with moss in them
Down in that neck of the country there
Around Houston and Galveston, Texas,
Where the flat lands run into the ocean
Called the Gulf of Mexico.
I flopped around in the ocean waters
And fought the sand fleas and mosquitoes
And got tired of that so I followed
A swarm of those mean biting flies
That suck the blood behind a dog's ear
And bite at the hoofs and heels of our cattle.
This took me up into a higher country
With deep gravel canyons running around

A country with a harder crust on the top of the ground
Called the west plains of Oklahoma
And the upper part of the panhandle of Texas
Where the irony grass sounds like
The reeds of a mouth organ in that wind
And where whole families of prairie dogs
And people dig down under the top sod
To chew and suck on the roots of grass
And on the Oklahoma side you find
Some cottonwood and elm trees stuck down around
The water holes and the creeks and low places
And you see some old tough bushes
All twisted and knotted and bent around
Trying to hold its roots under the soil
And its head up in that whipping wind
And then over on the Texas high side
It gets flatter and leveler
All in one big jump when you hit the cap rock
Down there around Clarendon
Or just in south of Jericho or Groom
Or just a little southeast of the Goodnight Ranch
A big cliff runs the length of that whole country
And the leaves of that upper plains grass
Is wiggling in a wind that's
Blowing thirty-six hundred feet high measured
From where a grass blade parts off from its first stem
This is that old upper plains
The old west plains some call it
And the creek and river beds are always dry
And the rabbits are always hungry
And the horses and cattle always hungry and thirsty
And the dogs always scared at the high winds
And everybody up there stays on
Some kind of a big high lonesome the biggest part of
Their time

Now back where I come from in Oklahoma
Its ground level was only six hundred feet
Above the level of the waters of the ocean
And this is the altitude around Okmulgee there,
And Henryetta, Seminole, Okfuskee, Weleetka,
Okemah, Buckeye, Castle, Clearview, Sand Springs,
Slick City,
I don't guess it was the good or the bad weather
That keeps you down in here or drives you out
As long as you can keep busy at your work
At some kind of a decent pay
But this is one mighty poor place to be
When you run out of anything to do
And nobody don't want you no more for nothing
And the signs all tell you to beat it
Keep a move on, high-tail it sister
And there just ain't no worse a spot
Nobody could be caught in than this
Strip of the country right in around here
Where the work plays out and you ain't needed
And I don't know why it is but it really
Is
And I don't know why it could be the worst
Part of the country but it mortally is
When the work's all over and the wind's blowed out
And the hard-handed people just wander about
When the big new sheriff with his thugs by god
Puts them use to be gamblers to tilling the sod
And you can't make a dime let alone get rich
It's a tough old titty, she's a mean old bitch
I always
Guessed it was mainly the fault of that
Low altitude of six hundred feet there above
The level of those ocean waters
Because there's not a place on God's green earth

No worse to get caught in broke and out of work
Than some kind of a country full of sandy hills
And that old brittle scrub oak and black jack
And thieving sheriffs and slick-finger deputies
God knows I hate them with all of my guts
I seen them rob more people and make more folks hungry
Than either the altitude or the weather either one
And this is why so many of us rambled out of there
And did get up over that cap rock of Texas
And up onto them upper plains and all out across there
But the weeds rolled around without no home
And the people rambled around the same as the tumble-
    weeds
And the people and the weeds are still out there tumbling
And the laws and the men in those offices out there
Run up and down those windy streets
Robbing and stealing and lying to one another
Just for a nickel or just for a dime to go down and buy
A drink of some kind of drinking whiskey or home brew
Or vanilla extract, or rubbing alcohol, hair tonic,
Or canned meat, or bay rum, or Jamaica Ginger, Jake,
Or lie and fight and rob just to get a dime or two
To lay like morning flowers over the nipples
Of the tits of some woman
And you might not exactly call her a whore
Because she is as good as the other folks out there
I wouldn't say that she was any better nor no worse neither
Than the best of the good ones nor the worst bad ones
Because men and the women here
Are just like the men and the women everywhere else,
Yes, if the nickels and the dimes they cheated one another
Out of was all laid rim to rim you would see a big new
Silver highway running from coast to coast eleven times
And a woman is woman enough to say
If all of the penisis I've had in my belly

Was taken out and laid down end to end
I suppose they'd reach from Nashville to Los Angeles.
I always did hope to meet as many people as I could
That was this honest about things as I hate to see
People that think one thing and tell you something else
And I always did hope that I never would get so
Narrow minded as to say that the country I come from
Is the best country of it all just because I come from it
I learned how to call those upper plains of west Texas
My home and my country just the same as those lower
Sand hills and scrubby trees down in Oklahoma
I think Oklahoma is as pretty and as nice a state as
You'll ever see and our sunsets are the best in the world
All of the travelers will tell you that. But I still
Hope that I can keep on liking all of this new country
I'm seeing all around me here, no matter where it is,
Because I don't never stand around and pant and sigh for
No stretch of country I done been through
And I don't bawl my eyes out for no special little bunch
Of the people that I met and got to knowing there
Because I see a new bunch just about every day now
Up here rambling around these big eastern cities
And I see their slums and back alleys and dangerous streets
And their kids that never did know what a breath of
Real fresh air was like in your nostrils
I won't even bother nor take time to tell what all
Different nationalities and colors they are
But I've heard so many poets and song singers
Waste all of their time harping about how their own
Little spot somewhere on the earth was prettier
And better and freer and happier and smarter than
All of the others
But I keep on going around and seeing places and people
And I've met them and slept with them and ate with them

And danced and sang with them from all four corners and
The middle sections of the country here and
It is all worth singing about and yelling about and
I don't blame you for having fits about how nice it was
Back somewhere in some little spot where you come from
But just don't be too quick to say that your little
Spot is any better or any nicer than all of the other
Little spots because everybody's eyes
Sees this same kind of a spirit and song in their own
Little bend in this big road through life
In the flat rocks and the round rocks of the desert
And in the muddy overflow of the flood basins
In the tangled vines and out of the songs of birds
And the wails and sighs and barks and yelps of wild animals
Everywhere
I learned this as I left that low Oklahoma country
And beat my way out up on top of those upper west plains
Of Texas

Kid

A kid is a thing that knows everything.

A kid is a thing that wants everything.

A kid is somebody that just don't want to stay still. A kid
chases all kinds of stuff. His pockets are trashboxes.

A kid throws down a ten-dollar toy and plays with an
old chunk of nothing.

Kids is looney. Kids do crazy things. Our wisest men and
women are still kids. Our geniuses never grow old, up a
little, but not old.

I paid two dollars to ride on a horse yesterday down along

woody Guthrie

1951

the beach for an hour. First horse I been astraddle of in ten years. My hipbone muscles feel like I'm an old stiffly crippler; outside of that, I'm just a kid up in my loft.

May 9, 1949

Rosh Hashonah

Today it's the first day of the New Year in Coney Island for the Jewish people.

And I guess its the same day for Jewish people all over everywhere.

Coney Island is a sight to see.

Our little corner grocery store is a wreck. Partly from that hurricane we had the other night, but mostly from these big crowds of people.

Men, and women and kids. The people know that the store will be closed for the next couple of days, and everybody has made a last minute rush to get a lot of things to eat and drink over the holiday.

My wife sent me after a few things, and I wrote it all down on a little card so I'd remember it. She looked all around the house and kitchen and told me what to write down. She gave me the money in the pocketbook and all of the point books.

And I got a good whiff of ocean air on the way over to the store.

Our little store is really a little one.

I had to stand around outside in a bunch of baby buggies, carriages, wagons, carts, bicycles, scooters, trikes, roller skates, ball bats, and families waiting.

One had come to the store out of each family and had

waited so long to get in that another one had come to find out what had happened to the first one. Then two more drifted down just to sort of see what was holding up the first two. Once in a while somebody would ooze out of the store door, but not often enough to talk about.

And somebody else would ease in. It would be more like it to say that when one would fight his way out with a sack and a bundle, nine more would hit the door like cattle stampeding in a thunder storm. But only one of us could get in.

Everybody laughed and talked about the New Year. We all had plenty of time to curse and swear and think up some more good New Year's Resolutions. A couple of women swore not to drink no more beer because it made them too fat. Three more swore not to eat no more candy nor cake. One skinny lady said she was going to take her malt and vitamin pills more regular.

There was a man that said, "I'm starting the New Year off ten cents in debt already!" A kid mumbled that he "would never smoke no more." A girl said, "If I can't drink and eat and smoke, what in the hell would I live for?" One lady bounced her little baby up and down in a buggy to put it to sleep. I said I didn't like it because she didn't put the kid to sleep, she only knocked him out. I said I seen this in the new doctor book we've got. She said, "And so whatta ya want me to do? Go and spend four dollars for some book that has run you out of your mind so soon?" A heavy-set lady shoved her way out of the door past us and I got knocked up against the plate glass window and was pinned there like a lost wrestler for several minutes. I tried to ootch my way over toward the door, but actually lost six or eight inches.

This is the first day of Rosh Hashonah, and people are buying all kinds of cakes, cookies, pickles, melons, loaves of bread, cheeses and meats, that remind them of the places back where they come from. Butter is hard to get and so is ketchup and canned fruits, but there's plenty of eggs, cheap beef, and green vegetables. Cases of noodles, kippered herring, matzoh, everything in the store is kicked and pushed around. Not because the man wants it to be, not because the people want it to be, but because this is the New Year and the war is on and the family that run the store can't get anybody to work for them. Store clerks are like waitresses nowadays, you can propose wedlock and matrimony, share the wealth, economic security and emotional rehabilitation, and bouquets and roses and a gay social life, and still, you don't get anybody to work for you.

Forty minutes rattle past me. I finally get inside. I don't know how I got there. Don't even ask me. It's worse in here than outside. Here, the air is stale and the smell of vinegar, cheese, floor sweep, cakes, pies, and all the things that are broken, spilled, and scattered around over the store. Milk bottles are tossed around everywhere. Empty soda bottles are under my feet. I can't look down because the men and women are so thick I can't bend my neck, but I can feel the bottles through the soles of my shoes and tell you the flavor of the soda that comes in them.

Everybody talks at everybody else and nobody listens to what anybody is saying. The store is moving and the walls are shaking inside and out. The plate glass windows rattle and sound like they'll break. I can't turn to either side because of the crowd and because of elbows, arms, shoulders, chins, and hat brims are in my face. I get up to the counter and am pressed so hard against it that the prints of my belt buckle will be there till the building falls down. I think, oh well, all of these Coney Island people were born and raised in these big crowds and they love the heaving and the pushing and the loud yelling just like cowboys or cottonpickers like to gang up somewhere and blow off their mouths. I hope I've still got that list of things the wife sent me with.

I've just made it up to where the lady behind the counter asks me what did I come for. She looks like a nice lady and so I try to tell her past four elbows and a couple of late autumn hats. She yells back that she is out of all of the things on my list and would something else be all right? I say okay and she sacks me up some things which are in close reach, and when it comes time for my points she says I owe her eight for a half a pound of butter. I feel around and have forgot the points at home on the dresser.

Ain't this a hell of a way to start off Yom Kipper?

Jacksonville Waltz (Sweet Jaxonville)

Jaxonville's a hard town . . . er maybe you don't know
They got cops that's eight foot tall
They tellya how to go . . .
They tellya how ya'd better walk
and where
and why
and when
And if ya don't alisten . . . it's the old jailhouse again!

Jaxonville's a mean town . . . maybe you didn't hear
Whiskey shot's a dollar
Eighty-five for beer
Jaxon breeds big barkeeps too
They're Southern White
and
Pure
They serve the white folks likker and black folks hoss
    manoor.

Jaxonville's a crap town . . . er maybe you can't see
They like their gamblin' better
Than a cockup drunkin' spree
They like those cards lots better
than ale
or beer
or wine
Those boys just better move along . . . they ain't no friends of
    mine.

Jaxonville's a tuff town . . . er maybe you won't hear
They gotta jail that's ten miles long
Once you get stuck off in there
you might
as well
be dead
You need ten U.S. Treasuries to take the pricetag off your
    head

Jaxonville's a WHITE man's town . . . maybe you don't know
Got no room for colored folks
SouthernwhiteJimCrow
So if your finger's itchy
To cop
a scalp
or two . . .
Theres lots of crackin' crackers that's game for me an' you.

Einstein Theme Song

Professor Albert Einstein has done as much if not more
than any other man to do away with bad race relations and
to set up some good ones. Maybe you don't believe this and
maybe he don't either, but it's a fact.

[191]

It seems to me like the farther down south you get the worse you see the colored races treated. But, when I say down south what do I mean, south of where, south of what, south of which? Well, the colored folks get treated just as bad up north, and just as miserable out west, and lots more of both back east.

This is because we stand around and let them draw all kinds of crazy boundary lines in between us and betwixt us. Somebody way up in a big high office has drawed a boundary line around every one of us and it keeps all of us cut off apart.

Einstein chopped down all of these crazy boundary lines for the next forty-nine billion trillion centuries to roll.

I'll tell you just how he done it.

He just proves to us that there ain't no such thing as east west north or south.

He says this world this earth here this planet we got borrowed is just one little wheeler here amidst many. Universes full.

He says this earth is about like a little rubber ball, and if you hold it up in your fingers like this and stick it all full of pins or hatpins, that, well, none of these pins will point to the east north south nor west. And of course he's right about that part of it, all right.

But he goes to prove and to figure and to show, too, that there ain't no sucha place as you could call up nor call down. No such a place as high nor low. Course you can see for your own eyes how this is the finest thing that's ever been proved since any of us jumped out of the bag. Us low folks don't have to look up to you high ones no longer starting out from here and now.

I tried here to write you a theme song, Mr. Einstein, for you to sing when you saw your fiddle at your lectures. And my theme song for you goes something like this:

If I cain't go east nor west,
If I cain't go north nor south,
I can still go in and out,
I can still go round and around;
    And around and around and around
    And around and around and around
    I can still go in and out
    And around and around and around.

Holding down Coney's Island
August, 1950

Einstein Brings Back Light Rays

I've wrongly been thinking for a few short centuries that when a ray of light leaves out from anywhere that, well, it's just a long time gone. It never does come back. Gone way over past Mexico way past over where the doggies go. I felt sad and blue and lonesome too just to think that I'd never ever see my ray of light anymore.

Just when I get friendly and all with a good social ray it hits the old trail called time and heads off out to the stirring waterlanes to never never be here with me any more. Which is a bad and a sad situation.

I'm glad to hear you say Mr. Einstein that my light ray does come back, a little bit bent up maybe, but better bent than to just not have no light ray at all. (In New England it's a toll.)

I'm sure glad to hear you and your pencil tell me that every light ray does bend, because, like you say, if they do take off on a straight beeline for that outer universe yonder they would just keep traveling in a straight beeline for nowhere and they never could come back here for me to look at. (And feel of.)

That stands to reason, don't it? It will stand to reason in the next few years to come that you and your pencil and your fiddle have brought back my rays of light to me. You caused me to get out here in my back yard and to look for them at least, which is a whole lot more than I've been doing since I thought the rays was all left out and gone and not to ever come back around here no more. I just got to where I quit looking for them. (These rays.) But, now that you have showed my thick skull that a light ray is just like everything else in this world and bends some, well, I have been out of my house and down along this beachysand here every morning around about sunup just to stand around and count the rays that drift in and see if there's any amongst them that I know by name or number.

You'd sure be surprised to hear that I have met and had a long chat with several rays as honest as they shine, and I've not only met up with rays which I know, but I've met up with little kid and baby rays that hatched out from rays that I used to vibrate around with. I tied a red radical ribbon on one ray and it vibed back just a few mornings ago. Which puts me away over on your side as a smart man. I guess that you and me would make about three smart men.

Old race hate, and just old greedy hate has darklit this planet so long now that we just cain't have too many good bright light rays on our side working and shining. You're the man that brought back all the lost light rays that will help us peace folks win this worlds war number three (and last).

Comes scientific socialism, Albert, every little kid among us will be out here riding around on one of these light rays you've brought back.

Old Buddy,
Woody Guthrie
August, 1950

In My Wildest Drunk Moments

In my wildest drunk moments I was thinking about some things that was for the good of the rest of you.

And in my odd and curious times, nervous and shaky times, I believe I thought lots of thoughts to help all of the rest of us.

I never did get wild enough, dancy enough, prancing enough, nor dopey enough to go around and say you ought to hate the race and color next to you there.

I go to your jail laughing at you simply because I know to my own soul that if your town was ruled and run by me and by my thoughts, tomorrow or the day after that, you would find everybody of each separate beautiful color holding hands and kissing new colors of babies into life on this grass and cement.

I sleep in your jail because I go around talking about the gospel of racial love and you would like to see me go around spreading and planting the gospel of racial hate.

I ride along sick and feverish here in this windborn boxcar because I talk the lingo of people loving one another and you would like to give me a big sack of your money to find more ways to go around talking and preaching all of the no good reasons why each one of us ought to hate and to fear and to tear into one another.

I am here to say now that life does not depend so much on what I drink as what I think. I see plenty of hateful, mean, ornery, bitter, sour and lost-out faces that spread the gospel of racial hate, yet they never taste a drink nor touch a drop, never rub a belly up against that deep soaked hardwood bar where we gang around and guzzle the brews. I

woody guthrie

guzzle many brews and ferments. I drink down odd con-
coctions, mixtures, stirs, and bubblings. I soak myself in
these same bubbles and foams that the rest of the race
stands around the drinking hole and drinks. I can't get full
enough of such sweet juice to hate you for the color of
your skin. I can't drink down enough, I've tried, I know, I
can't soak up enough to make me hate just broadside
wholesale in a lump sum your nose and slant of eye, your
lips, your hairs. I say again my drink did not boil off sad
and bitter bubbles of race hate. I felt in my warm blood a
kinder glow, a finer shine, a feeling of some lower higher
kinds.

I say that the man in me has done everything he seen the
rest of you wanting to do, and doing. The man in me done
like the man in you does. I did no more to the woman than
the woman asked me to do. I never did do anything to
any woman that she did not crave and cry in her soul for
me to do. And I've done to all women all kinds of things.
Only leaving out a few moves which I am terribly puzzled
about right this minute, I've done most everything with
most every sort and kind of a woman. And when your
women met me they tossed down their rails and their bars
and we did what we did to experiment and to try. To try to
find some new roll and twist, new smell, new taste, new
touch, new word, new song, new dance, new whispers in
the sun and by the moon, new things to make the rest
of us take up new strength and new nerve and to come to
one another in our new kinds of feelings and hopes. I never
spent an hour nor a night nor a day with any woman I
hated. I never slept with a woman I later joked about. I
never did sleep with a woman I cursed out later on. I gave
each woman all I had and she wanted for me to stay and
wept to see me go. I wept the same as she wept and I
weep but seldom about things. I was never any more
promiscuous than the capitalists made me. I was never any

looser nor wilder than your very own rules and laws made me. I never was any more upwards nor downwards than your own plans and lack of plans made me. I never broke any rule nor law that did not get in the way of my natural and native love and growing. I never paid any more girls to stay with me than paid me to stay with them. And when my kids get counted it will be a list long and tall, high wide and handsome, a list of names and faces that will give me whatever strength and power it takes to break out of every bilbo and shackle you and your phoney fears can tie around me.

I never did go off and drink and get drunk just because I wanted to think up some more ways to make people hate one another. I went off and got drunk, and still go off and get drunk, just in order to shake my head and to think and to dream up more and more ways to make folks love and like one another.

So, as far as drinking goes, I say, if you've found a woman of the caliber, tone, and the kind which I know, well, your eating, drinking, your fun having and your spree running is not going to do one half the damage to me and to my people that three words of racial and religious hatred is doing, has done. Go eat. Go dance. Go sing. Go drink. But let the sweet roll off from your tongue, and let words of family-style love and world-wide love come out from you.

March 3, 1947
Coney Island

Cathy Ann Guthrie

I sang for the UE Phelps-Dodge Workers down in Elizabeth, New Jersey, Sunday afternoon, February ninth. They had just won an eight months' strike, and Mario Russo had been killed a while back on picket duty. I left a note on our record player for Marjorie and Cathy that said, "Gone to Elizabeth, see you around the supper table. Your Pa."

Cathy had dressed up her prettiest that morning in her new pink dress, her own wooden beads, a little green hair ribbon, her new red sandals, some fancy socks, and had walked Marjorie over into Sea Gate a few blocks away to visit a while with Bubby and Zadie Greenblatt.

Marjorie and Cathy found my note on the record player when they got home about an hour after I had gone on the trolley car. It was a bright, warm, sunny day, with lots of people loafing along in the sun joking about going for a swim down on the beach.

Marjorie left Cathy sitting by the radio to answer the telephone if it rang. Cathy's job of answering the phone was something that tickled all of our friends as much as it tickled her. Marjorie ran across the street to buy some fruit and things, and ran back in about five minutes.

She found the hall filled with smoke and Cathy wrapped in a blanket the neighbors had thrown around her. She did not know exactly what had taken place. She grabbed Cathy up into her arms and carried her to the drugstore where the doctor gave her some kind of an emergency treatment while the fire engines and the ambulance came.

Cathy seemed to be in high spirits. Her clothing was burned off. Nobody could guess how bad she was hurt. The young Negro nurse in the ambulance was of such fine spirit that she kept hope and good feelings alive in Marjorie and in Cathy. Cathy laughed, joked, kidded, and sang to the nurse, and only told her Mommy, "Mommy, I burned up my new pink dress."

The kids from the buildings and houses around ran in ahead of the firemen and threw buckets of water onto the folding bed by the radio in the front room. This bed was the only thing burning in the house, but it made a terrible thick smoke such as smoldering cotton and straw throws off. This smoke must have blinded and strangled Cathy as she fought the fire to try in her own way to put it out, and caused her to push the front door shut tighter as she tried to get it open. The kids carried our things, my typewriter, our records, books, manuscripts, papers, our chest of drawers and other furniture out from the room where the blaze started. The firemen put the bed out, and tossed it out our back window into the yard. We will always thank all of you kids that ran in and saved our belongings from being ruined by the hoses and the axes of the firemen. We thank you firemen, too, since we know that your job is a rougher thing than arranging cut flowers in colored vases. We thank everybody.

Marjorie and several boys and girls from the neighborhood stood by Cathy's bed in the hospital and kept her company while the nurses and the doctors put on their wrappings and bandages. Cathy was clearly conscious from three that afternoon up to nine or ten that night, when she commenced to drift off into a coma of sleep caused by the drugs. The main job of Marjorie and the kids was to hold her foot and ankle where the blood transfusion tube was attached to the vein.

Cathy called off the name of every person she had ever known. She waved her bandages, sang, danced, laughed at her kids in her nursery school, teased all of her teachers, and put up a hard fight to overcome the burns. They told Marjorie that things were lots worse than they had figured at first, but that with Cathy's powers of resistance and fighting spirit, she could fight her way out and pull through. They had Marjorie sign a paper that said the mother knows that the child is in a very low and critical condition.

The Phelps-Dodge Workers had a free lunch of hot dogs and beer after their meeting was over to celebrate winning their strike. I grabbed a taxi to the Penn Station and rolled on back to New York. I bought Cathy a couple of toy balloons you blow up into a funny paper clown. I dropped by the office of Moe Asch of the Disc Company, and we talked over a few ideas for some more kids' albums of records across an eating table on Forty-Sixth Street. He gave me a dozen or so of some new little booklets of "Work Songs to Grow On" which I had illustrated and made up mainly by copying the drawings and the words of Miss Stackabones. I left Moe there at about ten-fifteen, grabbed the West End Subway and got home about eleven-thirty. Moe read about Cathy's accident on his way home, and called the Coney Island Emergency Hospital even before I got there.

I saw a note pasted on our front door that said, "Come to the Coney Island Hospital at once." I smelled the smells of smoke and ashes through our door, but had no key to open it up and take a look inside. Mrs. Shapiro and her sister in the front apartment told me, "There was a fire. Your little girl was burned. Go quick." I threw the two balloons and my books of kids' songs into Mrs. Shapiro's hands and ran out the door. I tried to picture in my mind what had happened. I thought Cathy had gotten into the burners of the cook stove. I saw her playing with books of matches on the bed. I told the cab driver all about it. He didn't know me from Adam, but he talked to me and kept me from going to pieces.

I met Marjorie in the hospital hall. She cried on my shoulders and told me that we had lost Cathy. I heard Cathy singing in her room and said she sounded like she had stuff enough to pull through anything. The nurses and the doctors commenced to change her wrappings just at this time and this was the worst of crying that Cathy went through. A few minutes later she was quietened down.

A newly married couple met me in the hall and cheered me up all they could. They were both worried about Marjorie on account of her being in her fourth month of a second baby. But Marjorie turned out to be the most solid and sane one in the whole bunch. She was like the hardest rock in the harbor. She still had on her red checkered house dress and her little red, white, and blue apron, and with her mouton coat hung across her shoulders. She told me, "No matter what happens, we've got to hold onto ourselves and to do things the way that Cathy would like to see us do."

We took our turns at holding Cathy's foot and ankle, at watching the drops of blood drip down through the hoses and tubes of glass from the pint bottles hooked in the metal rack. The nurses and the doctors were hard workers, fast, and several of them stood about the bed and did their jobs. We all agreed that the hospital staff did their very best to save Cathy's life, they treated us visitors and helpers with deep respect. They could not get a night nurse for us even though we did pay them eight and a half dollars to call the nurses over the phone. We called back to the little store here, Gunner's Candy Store, and they rousted more kids out of their beds who drove down to take their places at Cathy's bed while the rest of us grabbed little cat naps, drank hot coffee, and waited.

We saw all sorts of other patients come and go during the night. The benches were full at times with odd accidents. I heard one fellow tell the emergency nurse, "A little dog bit my hand." Another man told the night doctor, "A drunk chewed my right arm some." A lady had an infected scratch on her finger, got it wound up and left. The wind blew so hard outside that you had to throw your whole weight against the south door to get in and out. This was the snowiest and the coldest night so far this year. I could not get my hands on no warming stimulant, because the hour was so late and all of the luncheonette doors were closed. A big young husky ex-sailor by the nickname of Carrot Top brought a buddy of his down. Carrot Top was the favored boy friend of Cathy as well as our older daughter, Shirley Richman, that had the honor to be the first child watcher and sitter to Cathy Annie. Shirley's sister, Rozzy the Sea Girl, was the sweetheart of Carrot Top and of Cathy, too. Carrot Top stood more hours by Cathy's bed than any of the rest of us, because Marjorie was busy on the phone and I was busy watching Marjorie, and Marjorie was busy watching me. We let our hopes rise just a little speck as the night wore on, because, even there in her unconscious mind, Cathy kept on singing, dancing, teasing, ribbing, joshing in Yiddish dialect, in Oakie dialect, in every other dialect.

Three big specialists came in early the next morning and took a quick look at Cathy in her bed. The girl that held Cathy's foot was the new wife of Marjorie's brother, Mutt Greenblatt, an NMU merchant seaman, a chief engineer, who is now out to sea on a run to India and back. He met and married Clare in Liverpool, England, and it took them two whole years to get a passport across on an army transport ship, because of the highly progressive and revolutionary ideas of the both of them in regard to the fight between the worker and the boss man. Clare came like a cannon ball when Marjorie called her. Clare was one of the calmest and the strongest in the whole outfit, because she had driven an ambulance in England during the blitzes, and had seen lots of things like this, deaths, cryings, people lost and people weeping. She was there holding Cathy's ankle while the three big specialists looked through the bars of the bed and shook their heads. They called me out into the hall and told me to tell my wife that Cathy could not ever win the fight for life.

Marjorie called her mother in Sea Gate and told her the sad news, but told her not to come down unless she could bear her own self up, since we already had more than we could ever hold up. Marjorie's mother, Aliza Greenblatt, is one of the best known of Yiddish folk poetesses. She came down with her son, Cathy's Uncle Herb, and Cathy passed away while Clare held her foot and everybody else wept and cried out in the halls.

Some of them wanted to have a Jewish burial, some wanted a Catholic one, some liked some form of a Protestant funeral, but we turned the body over to the IWO for a quick and simple cremation to save several costly weeks of crying and weeping by peoples of every faith.

I broke in through the back window the next morning around about twelve o'clock, and walked all around through the house looking for the cause of the fire. It was not the cook stove, because the kitchen showed no signs of it. It was not my books of paper matches, because the box of them had not been touched on their shelf. It was, as Marjorie told me in the hospital, an electrical cord from the wallplug to the newly rebuilt radio. Flames had made but one little mark in the whole house, and that was where the radio lead wire had got hot and burned in two. The wire ran down in behind the bed from the wall to the radio. The radio was not playing. It was the newest wire in our house, since we'd had it rebuilt by a man down the street just a few months ago. He had used some sort of a synthetic wartime wiring of a cheap and easy sort that had sparked, shorted, and blazed up to catch the bed sheets, blankets, spread, and Cathy's dress as she fought to put it out.

Arthur Young, a sixteen-year-old boy living just above us, by some streak of fate happened to walk in at the door. He saw the smoke boiling from our door, and bursted in to find Cathy crying and screaming, trying to get out to her Mommy. He yelled up the stairs to his brother and friends taking a bath, and they grabbed pails of water which they threw onto the bed. Arthur's bravery and clear head was told about in several newspaper stories. He was a real hero. He said that a buddy of his passed through the hall a minute or so before him, saw the same smoke, heard Cathy crying for help, but just did not know what to do about it. His buddy went on up the stairs to the Young apartment, and Arthur stepped in a minute or so later. He got the grey wool blanket from the neighbors and wrapped Cathy up in it. Marjorie found all of them in the hall in this fashion.

I am writing this because I want our uncounted and unnumbered friends to know the whole thing from start to finish. Every neighbor said that Marjorie was gone for less than five minutes, that the whole thing struck in three or four minutes. And this faulty radio wiring was the one thing, the only thing in our whole house which we had not expected, had not told and warned Cathy about. Phone calls, letters, cards, telegrams, checks, presents, have been piling in. Cathy's smile and her spirit spread everywhere she went. Teachers wrote in to say that Cathy was the happiest of all the kids in their nursery school. Folks that dance and sing to Cathy's songs on records wrote, called, wired us. We told all of them that we had no intention of letting such a wild accident get us down nor to keep us down in spirit, that we aimed to go right on and to have our next several babies in the same progressive and social-minded ways which we raised Cathy on. Cathy was a citizen here, a full-fledged voter, her voice and her ideas ran this house here, ran our careers, ran our works, gave us our best thoughts, visions, ideas, plans. The house is all cleaned up now because of the way our friends knelt down and scrubbed on their knees. Cathy's drawings are still here on our walls, her trinkets, toys, her letters, her gifts and presents for the new baby inside of Mommy's tummy, all of them are here. We boxed up her usable toys and gave them to the nursery school. Her clothing we gave to the office of the Communist Party here to pass on to needier kids. A friend planted a tree in her honor somewhere in the Holy Land around Palestine. Cathy made a big donation both in spirit, feelings, as well as in good ores and materials during her four short years here amongst us.

We thank all of you that felt this sad accident with us. You who visited our house here in Coney. You that called. You letter writers. You that did none of these things, but just felt for us an honest or a deep feeling. Cathy sang and danced right up to the last, and we know that she would like for her Mommy and her Daddy to feel this same way. So, let's not feel low and lonely like we might like to feel, but let's feel high and mighty like Cathy would ask us to feel. Let's take faith in her four big happy years, and let's keep on singing and dancing at our Hootenannies and at our nursery schools and in our studios, the way Cathy would like for us to do.

And let's keep on marching and fighting, too.

Cup of Coffee

A cup of coffee is a thing to be drained but never to be trusted.

It warms your lip and flops your tongue, rains on your throat and your belly and warms you for a short visit

It tickleth thy pride

It puffeth up thy false hopings

It restoreth nothing

It promises much and delivers but little

A cup of coffee is much like the woman you wedded but never did mind

It gives rise to foamy floats of plans that get you up from your night of sleep to write down the truth about nothing

It warms your friendship for a brief gab and runs off to the cellar

Coffee costeth per cup a five-cent piece which surely is to the merchant trader four and one half cents pure profit

When drunk cold it drives you from your home

When drunk lukewarm it brings you to vomit

When boiling hot it raises sores on your tongue

It fades and dims before it turns the next bend in your bloody vein

It is never there when you want it

It never makes you do what you really want it to do

It confoundeth great mathematicks

It lives up to no slogan

Its bubbles themselves are brown bitter lies

Coffee is a renegade and a deserter

Coffee is a holdback and a rock in the road

Coffee loads and sinks the hulls of pretty fair ships

And could be grown in big enough batches to drown the human race in its juice

It costs a penny for a spoonful and is not worth two pennies for a trainful

Yet, I run for it by the mile, and drink it hot before I read my papers of the morning's rapings

Two cups I drink if the news is extry hot

I swim, and I float on the crazy skum of a saucer of stainful coffee

I trust my very existence to the stuff a dozen times a day, and it never gives back, not one silly penny

Coffee is something that is here to stay and to stay longer than I will

But I had to tell you about it

So that you could drown yourself in my same saucer.

Coffee Jake
Sunk Here
May 30, 1949
CI NYC

To People's Songs

My Hootenney
(Over-written with—My Hooten Anny)
Hootenanny! Hootenanny!

Hootin' Annie! Hotting Anny!
Long might you pull and take breath
Here in the midst, Hootenanny! Sweet Hootenanny!
Sounding sweeter to me than any honey in any rock!
Hoot out to my world your clear young pretty voice
And sing to my scared and my nervous cowards
How easy is the union way of life
How nice and warm the union side of life;
How big and bright and sparkeldy is the lovingside
Of my big union world out freed from your fearful shadows;
Hootenanny Man! Holler these things to them!
Hottennanny Daddy! Hoot out at your greedy enemy
Greed itself and shout and joke and sing
Down into the gutters and drains of history,
Down into the fires of old creation,
Down under, down in under, done done whittled on down;
Fiddled on down, all of my worst enemies;
Riddled on down, all of my worst cowards;
Jazzed right on down, all of my old strangly notions;
I could call you my hottenanny,
Or I could call you my shootenanny, scootin' Anny,
Of my squirtin' Annie, or my squeekenannie,
My flirkinanny, flippinanny, shipinannie,
My flirtinanny, whoopinanny, scoopinanny,
And I'd still be okay as far as your name goes;
I did help to think up that name, hotinanny,
To mean the place where you could come to and to
Yell your head off about what's eatin' on you;
Tell wh's beatin' on you, mistreatin' on ya;
Stoolin' on ya, droolin' on ya, tomfoolerin' on ya;
So's you'd have a good place to come sing and dance
About whoever it was that done you wrong and howly;
Sing about who it was robbed you, ribbed you, gypped ya;
Rifled ya, stiffled ya, pilfred ya, zypphered ya;
Shot y', got y', what notted y', spotted y',

Goodfed ya, spoofed ya, spondoolyxed ya, bamboozled ya;
Damnfoozled ya, rubberhozed ya, bloodynozed ya;
Hypoed ya, wheedled ya, needled ya, bloodnozed ya;
Hypoed ya, wheedled ya, needled ya, tweedled ya;
Hypoed ya, wheedled ya, needled ya, tweedled ya;
Hurt ya, scaped ya, raped ya, faked ya, trymaked ya,
Manhandled ya, eggscrambled ya, fandangled ya, misdone
   ya
Badmanaged ya, hotcabbaged ya, booted ya, tooted ya, hot-
   footed ya
Insulted ya, hotcabbaged ya, booted ya, tooted ya, hotfooted
   ya
Insulted ya, cursewordled ya, bemuddled ya, muddied ya;
Unzippered ya, unlaced ya, traced ya, fastraced and fast-
   talked ya
Bilboed ya, badshowed ya, sadroaded ya, throwed ya,
   blowed ya;
Badtimed ya, lastdimed ya, frothyslimed ya;
Sweet Hootenanny Girl, sweeter than all of these war shakers
Sweeter to me than all of them quickers and takers and
Lossey tongued fakers; you are prettier than a million
Of their happytwisters and greast sisters twitching it for a
   war;
You are pitching it for peace, Hootenanny Girl,
You are frailing it for friendship, Hootenanny Lady Fair;
Tossing it for the boss ain't your kind of a wine dance, is it?
You do the fine dance about humanly sisterhood;
You do that finer dance about neighborly nippyloving;
Making love is ten jillions better than shaking up a war;
Making your peace is better than the wargirl's crazy greases;
You'll forget more about pretty things than she ever will
   know;
Hootenanny Girly. Hootenanny Pearly. Hootenanny Maidela.
You can sing and talk all eternity about who treated your
   folks bad.

I was just born alisting to all you hootenanny heartsongs,
And I was born here to listen, to linger and to lay and to
Play and to pray and to dance around my atom fire as much
  as I
Dang please while you're singing out the sounds of your
Hootennanny song. We found together the only good way to
Spend the long and the short time of life, didn't we Huhhh?
Didn't we, Sugar? Diddlent we Babe Oh Bab?
Shootin' it at th' Hootenanny!
Bootin' it at the Skootenanny!
Rakin' it at the Skweekinanny!
Takin' it at the Bawlin' Squaller! Huh? Didn't we?
Us? I mean, I mean, you and me here!
Up here hootin' it off together!
Hootin' it, rootin' it, knockin' it,
Rockin' it, sockin' it, boxin' it, and a foxin' it;
Skippin' it, and a hippin' it here at our big loud Hootenanny;
Hoofin' our hearts down to a nub here at our Hoofinanny;
Hoopin' it, hopin' it, slappin' it, tappin' it,
Groovin' it, greazin' it, shovin' it, freezin' it,
Dreamin' it, schemin' it, fussin' it and a cussin' it,
Frettin' it and a sweatin' it out, here, here at this very
  hootenn
Mopin' it and a hopin' it, softshoein' it softsoapin' it;
Hopin' it, hopin' it, hopin' it, hoppin' it;
Hopin' this whole damn crazy warry world will drop
Down all of its sad shooting irons and killing kannons
And come with you and me and slip it
Flip it over into that good groove we love so well;
That good old groove of world work, world peace, world
  kissing;
Worlds all hootin' it, hopin' it,
Dreamin' it, screamin' it, frimmin' it, frammin' it;
Whoppin' up a heaty pitch of firey kissfyrnaces which no
Uramyuuum stockypile could hit on a trillion generations;

Me'n you's
Got the old world by the horn, ain't we, Babeyy?
Didin't we grab things by the hot end, Friend?
Huhhh? You an' me did, both did, diddle we?
Hippin' it here;
Slippin' it here;
Drippin' it here at our Hootenanny?
I can't quite clear just quite remember how it went that other
Time
When we
Scooped it at that Heatin' anny,
Can you?
Not quite.
Not plum quite.
I think we gotta go and try back over it
Once more/won't you/don't you/Hittenanny?/Hootenanny?
        /Hooten/At our/Hootenanny?/Yeahhhhh!

Gene Debs

Every hand that did worry very much about how to best
help the folks that do the hard work in this world and around
this world has wrote down the name of Gene Debs, or spoke
about Gene Debs or sung some song about Gene Debs.

Gene Debs is a pure cross between Jesus Christ and Abe
Lincoln. A lover. A man to think. A man to fight. A man to
work hard and a man that loved hard work and hard workers.

The courtroom didn't scare Gene Debs. The jailhouse
didn't scare him, either, neither did the ash pile, nor the

grave. He gave every earthly thing several times every day over to the labor union movement which was his religion.

And he died easy like a man in high peace.

August 4, 1948
Coney on the dry sand
long time back.

To That Man Robert Burns

To that man Robert Burns
Dear Robert Burns,

You skipped the big town streets just like I done, you ducked the crosstown cop just like I ducked, you dodged behind a beanpole to beat the bigtime dick and you very seldom stopped off in any big city where the rigged corn wasn't drying nor the hot vine didn't help you do your talking.

Your talking was factual figures of the biggest sort, though. Your talking had the graphboard and the chart and had something else most singers seem to miss, the very kiss of warm dew on the stalk.

Your words turned into songs and floated upstream and then turned into rains and drifted down and lodged and swung and clung to drifts of driftwood to warm and heat and fertilize new seeds. Your words were of the upheath and the down, your words were more from heather than from town. Your thoughts came more from weather than from schoolroom and more from shifting vines than from the book.

I go to the church halfway between the farm and halfway

[213]

into the town and halfway back. I sing and dance at just one altar only and cry with the folks that would like to be more fertile. If there's a bench I kneel down to laugh and cry on, I suppose it's this bench with the kids waiting along it while us dads and us mamas stamp and stomp around looking for something to give our trip more sense. I worship in the limbroof arbors of pure fertility and very little else makes sense to me. Like Robert Burns and Jesus and some others I believe we'd ought to learn how to make a law or two to help us brothers love the sisters more.

I bought your little four-inch square book while I was a torpedoed seaman walking around over your clods and sods of Glasgow and the little book says on the outer cover, Fifty Songs of Burns, the price, 4d, and I read from page to page and found you covered a woman on every page. I thought as I picked the book up here at home that maybe the book had ought to have some kind of a new name. Like, Fifty Pages Fifty Women, enlarged upon by Robert Burns.

Well, Rob, it's awful rainy here in Coney today. Been drizzling like this now for several days to make some folks happy and some folks sad, since this is a big resort town and folks pay good money to come here from all over. Some like the rain today and some folks hate it. I like it and love it for several reasons, like you'd love it, to see our new seeds grow in this old trashy back yard, and to see these green shoots, roots, limbs and leaves start dancing like Tirza and her Wine Bath. And because Marjorie and me just painted some flowers of a wild and jumpy color on our pink wall of the baby's room so when he does squirm his way out here to see his light of the day he'll see some twisting flowers like you seen all around your rock hearths and heatherhills there all over your Scotland. This rain is making the grass and flowers spud out, the roots to crawl like guerrillas, and the house to take a better shape, so's our little shoot and shaver can have these growing limbs to give him such a good fast start that maybe he can grow up in four years with us giving him pushes to be as happy and dancy and glad and joking and pretty as our little Stackybones was on that Sunday's afternoon when she got dressed up her very prettiest in her pinkiest dress and greenest ribbon to look just as nice and sweet and glad and pretty as any of your fifty girls you raved about. And fifty times fifty. The only good part of living you really did miss, Bob, was not to get to stick around a house like Marjorie keeps and see a kid like Cathy dance and grow. You died at thirty-four which was a bit too young for you to get to see these things I'm seeing in the faces of my kids.

This is why I'll keep you posted and brought up to date as the year leafs out and me and Marjorie have more kids of the kinds you missed out on.

June 9, 1947

My People

My people
Are not quaint
They're not colorful
They ain't odd nor funny nor picturesque,
Nor strange,
Nor humorous,
And they're not strangers
You introduce with big long words.

I don't know
And won't say what my people are
Just folks
Just like me
All messed up and tangled up
And all worried
And all screwed up.

I wouldn't say
And I couldn't say
That they are under the name of any big long word
Because any big long word
Would not fit nobody I know
Wouldn't tell you who nor what
My people really are.

It makes me sore to hear or to see or to read
How you big long-haired writers
Whack away at my people
Chew and cut and saw away at my people
Grind and drill and whittle away at them
Trying to make out like you are their Savior
Or their way shower
Or their finder
Or their discoverer
Like Balboa, like Colombo, like Lincoln
Discovering the people
Discovering the people like an island
Or finding them like some continent
Setting your sails and your compasses
And setting your maps and your charts and your pens,
And stumbling onto my people
Like they was some sort of a new piece of land
Sticking up out of an old body of water.

I can't find no long word to call them
And I can't find no reason to make a puzzle about them,
No excuse for not talking for them and about them,
No reason for hiding my fear in the pages of proverb books,
Dictionaries, good and bad books,
Bibles, histories, language books, and other books.
I won't say that I found any of my people in these books,
But I did lose several of them there,
In these books,
And under these covers,
And between these pages.
But I won't charge the human race several thousand dollars
Just to make up long words to tell you
Which book we lost our people in,
Nor which book to go to
To look for my people again in.

I've found women passionate
As women can be
But never yet found the woman
Passionate enough for me.

Most Times

Most times
When I catch myself
Thinkin about you
An
Thats
Most times

[218]

Seems like
I wanta get it out
Some way
Just
Sorta
Someway

I get to just lookin around
At things you laid your hand on
An course
I guess
I'm one
Of them things

Some how
Or another
I figure I'm kin
Some kin or another
To
Every single one
Of everything you ever laid your hand on

Naturally I
Suppose
You feel this here same way
About somebody
Or another
Somewheres

So
Sorta works out that
Everybody feels some kin
To everything anybody ever laid hands on
And made

Or built up
Or fought and died
To live
And keep

Most poems is
Over
Before
You know it

Only main trouble with poetry is it leaves too much blank
space on every page

W N E W

Well, I sorta got to rush along here. I got a big lot of stuff
to do in a very short time. Fifteen minutes. But the men
that run this radio station told me that if you write me
enough cards and letters that they'd stretch my time out and
make it thirty minutes.

I've followed all kinds of big work jobs all over the
country, like the oil fields, coal mines, big timber jobs, the
Grand Coolee Dam, the TVA in the state of Tennessee, the
harvesting of all kinds of crops like cotton, wheat, spuds,
beets, and grapes and fruits and berries and vegetables. I've
followed the building of the big highways like the Lincoln
and the Sixty-Six. And the hard rock tunnels and the WPA
roads and streamlined speedways, and the building of the
big ships, and the places where ferryboats land and where
the subway trains and all of the other trains load up full of
people, and I sang in road houses, hotels, messrooms,
churches, union halls, saloons and night clubs and taverns,

and have always sung for twelve or fourteen hours a day and sometimes twenty-four. And now to try to sing these same kinds of songs on a little old fifteen-minute spot here on the radio, well, it cramps me just a little bit. Sort of slows me down. I ain't got elbow room. Ain't got room enough to breathe in.

I need thirty minutes at the very least. If you write me a card or a letter, then the owner will see that you want thirty minutes, too, and then we'll be getting something done.

I sing all kinds of tales and stories that the people sing while they work or while they're looking for work. I sing old-time songs about love and fights and so forth and so on, and about the big jobs that have made this country what it is.

I don't sing any songs that are not real. I don't sing any silly or any jerky songs, nor any songs that make fun of your color, your race, the color of your eyes or the shape of your stomach or the shape of your nose. I don't sing any songs of the playboys and the gals that get paid for hugging the mikes and wiggling their hips. I sing songs that people made up to help them to do more work, to get somewhere in this old world, to fall in love and to get married and to have kids and to have trade unions and to have the right to speak out your mind about how to make this old world a little bit better place to work in. I sing songs about people that are fighting with guns to win a world where you'll have a good job at union pay, and a right to speak up, to think, to have honest prices and honest wages and a nice clean place to live in and a good safe place to work in. I even sing songs about getting nursery schools for little kids too young to play in the streets, and schools where all of the other kids can go to keep from playing their games under the garbage trucks. I don't sing any songs about the nine divorces of some million-aire playgal or the ten wives of some screwball. I've just not got the time to sing those kind of songs and I wouldn't sing them if they paid me ten thousand dollars a week. I sing the songs of the people that do all of the little jobs and the mean and dirty hard work in the world and of their wants and their hopes and their plans for a decent life.

I happen to believe that songs and music can be used to get all of these good things that you want. Maybe you never did hear a song that you figured was of much help to you in getting the job and the pay and the mate and the home that you want. Maybe you never did hear a song that you thought was a help to you in paying off your debts.

I hate a song that makes you think that you're not any good. I hate a song that makes you think that you are just born to lose. Bound to lose. No good to nobody. No good for nothing. Because you are either too old or too young or too fat or too slim or too ugly or too this or too that. . . . Songs that run you down or songs that poke fun at you on account of your bad luck or hard traveling.

I am out to fight those kinds of songs to my very last breath of air and my last drop of blood.

I am out to sing songs that will prove to you that this is your world and that if it has hit you pretty hard and knocked you for a dozen loops, no matter how hard it's run you down nor rolled over you, no matter what color, what size you are, how you are built, I am out to sing the songs that make you take pride in yourself and in your work. And the songs that I sing are made up for the most part by all sorts of folks just about like you.

I could hire out to the other side, the big-money side, and get several dollars every week just to quit singing my own kind of songs and to sing the kind that knock you down still farther and the ones that make fun of you even more, and the ones that make you think that you've not got any sense at all. But I decided a long time ago that I'd starve to death before I'd sing any such songs as that. The radio waves and your jukeboxes and your movies and your song books are already loaded down and running over with such no-good songs as that anyhow.

I leave it up to you to write in to me. Write in and tell me what you think. Get your whole family and your friends and your neighbors to write in. Tell me that you think such a program should be more than fifteen minutes long.

Or tell me that you don't like my songs. Tell me why you don't like them. Tell me why you think they should not be heard on the air at all. Tell me to go jump into the East River or to take a high dive off the top of the Empire State Building. But write. Write right now.

Tell me something.

You can be three years old or two years old or you don't even have to be one day old. Just so you can write. Just so you can hold up a pen or a pencil or punch at the keys on a typewriter. Write. Write two words or two million. You can be seventy-five years old or a hundred and seventy-five or you can be as old as the forks in the road or the wrinkles in the hills. But write. Write right now.

I sing religious songs. I sing union songs. I sing all kinds of songs about people that are supposed to be mean, or vulgar, low down, no money, no good, and I sing songs that tell who the racketeers are and how they rob you and how they work and how they would like to keep you as their slave. And I sing the songs about robbers and about outlaws and people that try to take it from the rich and give it to the poor. I sing songs that tell you just why you can't help the people that are poor just by grabbing a club or a knife or a gun and going out to be an outlaw. I sing songs about the outlaws that the people loved and the ones that the people hated. I sing any song that was made up by the people that tells a little story, a little part, of our big history of this country, yes, or that tells a part of the history of the world.

The folks all around the world have been fighting now for a hundred centuries to all be union and to all be free and I sing the songs that tell you about that. I tell you about the hired thugs and the hired sluggers and the gas-bomb deputies.

I tell you the tall tales of the champion workers and the fights they had to see who could do the most work. I tell you the tales of the world's champion drinkers and the world's champion thinkers and the world's champion horses and the best argufiers and shooters of the bull. I tell you about the fastest horses and the fastest lovers and the biggest eaters and the fastest travelers.

I tell you about the soldiers and the sailors that are fighting and singing and winning this better world a coming and I tell you about the people here and everywhere that are working and singing and fighting to back up the men in the armed services.

I tell you about everything in the world and on the world and above the world and about the world as well as around the world and through the world and in the world and near the world. I tell you about the winds and the weathers and the oceans and the lands and the continents that have riz and sunk since this little hunk of dirt first whirled off of the burning sun. I tell you of the men and the women that bathed their eyes in the zig zag lightning and hugged and kissed in the rumbling thunder and about every union wheel that ever did run down a union road or down a union rail and every puff of union smoke that ever did riz up out of a big high union smokestack.

These are just a few of the little things that I'll tell you. These are just a few of the little minor details. But what I need is thirty minutes. Not fifteen. But thirty. Not sixteen or seventeen or eighteen or nineteen. But a whole big thirty minutes so I'll have room enough and time enough to at least take a deep breath and expand my chest and so's I'll not feel rushed and cramped up. Fifteen minutes insults me and it insults the hundred million folks for which I speak.

I speak for the union people that see a union world and that fight for a one big union all around the world. I speak as a singer for the AF of L, CIO, Brotherhoods and Sisterhoods and all of the kids and childhoods and all of the other hoods but I fight against the white hood of the Ku Klux Klan because I hate them and their gizzards and their whizzards and their lizzards and I hate their hot tar and their feathers and their beatings and killings and hangings of union men and women all over the country. I speak for the human beings of this human race and when anybody quits being a human and goes to fighting against the union right then I jump on them with all of my teeth and toenails. And I grab me a root and I growl. And I hang on and I keep on singing and yelling and singing and yelling and singing and yelling and reading and writing and hollering and fighting and everything else.

So if you're on my side which is the union side which is the human side then set down right now and write to me and say; Dear Woody, Station WNEW: I'm for you. You need thirty minutes in which to have elbow room.

Or if you're against me. Well, write. Write and tell me all of the reasons that you can think of why you hate my guts. Tell me how bad I sound and how I can't play and how I never could sing and how I never will be able to talk. And how I can't even think straight. Tell me that I had ought to get off the air. And tell me to go out and jump off of the sharp point of the Statue of Liberty. And I'll read your letter over the air and I'll most certainly tell you to go and do the same thing.

> Write me in your card or letter
> Send me in your telegram

Tell me I'd oughta have thirty minutes
Or tell me I'm worth a tham.

December 3, 1944

The Dying Doctor
or
The Company Town Doctor

Doctor Leo Hayes was our company doctor
From the big coal company he got his pay
For thirty-nine years he tried to cure us
And now today on his deathbed lay.
He called his five boys and his three daughters
And at his bed we stood around
We heard him tell the history of the coal miners
And he said, "Don't let these people down."

You are all connected with the practice of medicine
You promise you'll keep true I know
You will do your best to help these people
I close my eyes for I must go.
His youngest girl was Doctor Betty
With her face so pretty and her smile so sweet
She walked the coal towns of Force and Byrndale
She saw the sewage waters flowing down the street.

She saw the children drink the cankered water
She saw the chickens fly up on the roof
She saw the waters overflow the sewers
And flood their gardens of victory.

She went to the big shots of the Shawmut Company
She did not beg and she did not plead
She stood flatfooted and pounded the table
Sewer pipes and bathrooms are what we need.

My daddy told me to fight to cure sickness
But I can't cure sickness with sewage all around
These germs kill people quicker than I can cure them
We need a foundation under every house.
We need a bathroom for every family
Yes, you can set there and blink your eyes
Three hundred miners are out behind me
We will clean this town up or know the reason why.

I quit my job as the company doctor
I nailed up my shingle and went on my own
I carried my pillbag and waded those waters
I set by a deathbed in many a home.
I saw you catch rainwater in rusty washtubs
I saw you come home dirty up out of your pits
Watched you ride with your coffin up to your graveyard
With not a nickel to pay your burying debt.

On July the fifteenth from the hills around
Three hundred miners walked down through town
The state inspector was testing the water
While he was working you stood around.
One miner asked him to have a drink free
The inspector looked out toward our pits
He set his hat back on his head and says,
"I wouldn't drink a drop of that on a bet."

I think of my daddy and brothers and sisters
When we stood around his dying bed
When I walk the streets of the company towns

I can hear every word my daddy said.
The Shawmut Company is caught in its own paws
The people not worth the money they cost
A hundred have died, three hundred not working
Thirty thousand tons of coal is lost.

September 9, 1945

The Blinding of Isaac Woodard

(Tune: "The Great Duststorm")

My name is Isaac Woodard, my tale I'll tell you;
I'm sure it'll sound so terrible you might not think it true;
I joined up with the Army, they sent me overseas;
Through the battles of New Guinea and in the Philippines.

On the 13th day of February of 1946
They sent me to Atlanta and I got my discharge pin;
I caught the bus for Winsboro, going to meet my wife,
Then we were coming to New York City to visit my parents
    both.

About an hour out of Atlanta, the sun was going down,
We stopped the bus at a drugstore in a little country town;
I walked up to the driver and I looked him in the eye,
"I'd like to go to the washroom, if you think we got time."

The driver started cursing and then he hollered, "No!"
So, then I cussed right back at him, and really got him told.
He said, "If you will hurry, I guess I'll take the time!"
It was in a few short minutes we was rolling down the line.

We rolled for thirty minutes, I watched the shacks and trees,
I thought of my wife in Winsboro waiting there for me.
In Aiken, South Carolina, the driver he jumped out;
He came back with a policeman to take me off the bus.

"Listen, Mr. Policeman," I started to explain,
"I did not cause no trouble, and I did not raise no cain."
He hit me with his billy, he cursed me up and down,
"Shut up, you black bastard"; and he walked me down in
    town.

As we walked along the sidewalk, my right arm he did twist;
I knew he wanted me to fight back, but I never did resist;
"Have you your Army discharge?" I told him, yes, I had;
He pasted me with his loaded stick down across my head.

I grabbed his stick and we had a little run, and had a little
    wrastle;
When another cop run up with a gun and jumped into the
    battle;
"If you don't drop that sap, black boy, it's me that's dropping
    you."
So I figured to drop that loaded sap was the best thing I
    could do.

They beat me about the head and face and left a bloody trail
All down along the sidewalk to the iron door of the jail;
He knocked me down upon the ground and he poked me in
    the eyes;
When I woke up next morning, I found my eyes were blind.

They drug me to the courtroom, and I could not see the
    judge;
He fined me fifty dollars for raising all the fuss;

The doctor finally got there but it took him two whole days;
He handed me some drops and salve and told me to treat my-
    self.

It's now you've heard my story, there's one thing I can't see,
How you could treat a human like they have treated me;
I thought I fought on the islands to get rid of their kind;
But I can see the fight lots plainer now that I am blind.

I wrote this ballad on the 16th day of August in the year
1946, one block from the wreckage of the Atlantic Ocean, on
the beach at Coney Island, New York.

Let Me Go

Let me go to my home in my faraway West
To my family and friends and my folks I love best
Where my hightoppy trees wave and my sweetwaters flow
Let me go old slaverdriverman let me go.

Let me walk t' my place where my wildriver flies
Here where I roamed in my young boyhood days
My good mother's heart for me will overflow
Let me go you old slave driver man let me go.

I'll walk back to my Daddy and talk at his side
Just like I walk'd back in my manhood and prime
I'll trap my good deermeat my deer and my doe.
Let me go you old slavey driver man let me go.

I'll go breathe in some more of my coldmountain air

Thru all of my hills and my valleys so fair
In my darkydeep forest I'll make arrows and bows
Let me go you ol' slaveydriver man let me go.

I'll walk back and meet my true darkeyed girl
Like she taught me how back in my talltree world
She loves like my fawn and as pure as my snow
Let me go you old slaveydriver man let me go.

I never willt stray from my deep forest home
When my sore toes once more back they roam
Till my dyin day comes I wont leave it no more
Let me go you ol' slaveydrivery man let me go.

Looks Like It's Here

Well it's here. The thing we've all been waiting for.
Ever since men have been men
The thing they've all been watching for and looking for
And waiting and working for is now here.
You can announce it. That's all it needs.
Just being announced.
Just told around that it's here.
Because it's been on its way
Ever since there was a breath of life climbing out of the mud
Of evolution or a meat-eater chasing down its meat.
Or a caveman shaking apples out of a tree with a stick
And wondering what made them all fall down to the ground.
Yes. The apes and the gorillas and the monkeys barked
And the hyenas in the underbrush trotted in packs
And laughed and slit throats and got swallowed by big
   snakes

Because it seems like the monkeys and the snakes
And the yelping hyenas and men
All were looking for the same thing
And all going after it in their own ways:
Running and fighting and making a stand
Hiding and trapping and tilling the land
They've been feeling the call of freedom in their bellies
And the electricity of freedom shocking in their scalps
Because that feeling of freedom
That feeling
Is about all of the life there is here
Or ever was
Or ever will be.
It's the weather acting up
And it's everything that seems to fight everything else
But the funny part is that
The whole thing was just hunting life
And work is the only rest in life
And freedom is the only thing worth working for
Or being here for in the first place
Or talking about
Or singing about
Or dancing about
Or fighting a war about.
What is this business called freedom?
Freedom is the right to get together
And to work for each other instead of against each other
And that's why
The freedom side
Little by little
Little at a time
Has always won every battle
And will keep on winning—
Will keep on living
Because life is freedom

And without either one you don't need the other
They're one and the same thing.

October 18, 1942

My Oklahoma

I can't hardly make your house out from the window of my plane. It's not stormy down between us. I can't see the tracks of rain.

The lady tells me friendly we're up over my home state, Oklahoma, but I can't see anything down there that looks like my Oklahoma to me.

The gyro says ten thousand foot above the level of the sea. That flatty flitter just don't look like Oklahoma much to me.

Two-fifty every hour that's how fast our shadow flies from the sun down cross the creek there. Did you hear us way up here? Did my shadow taste the ragweed and the gypsum in your yard?

Couldn't see no red nor grey clay which I beat on School House Hill. In that big deep floody ditch down School House Hill. Cain't talk much. Cain't rub jaws for long—at 250 an hour, ten thousand spans up in the sun. Can I?

July 31, 1949

I'll Not Beg

I'll not beg nobody
I won't beg nobody
I'll sing just how I feel

And I'll work
But I'll not beg anybody nor nobody
I'll just tell it
The ways I seen it
And how things is
And what caused it
And what's good
And what's bad
And how to fix it
And you can help
Or you can stand there and just gawk
And you can go ahead on sleeping
And you can even beat me up
And you can poke your fun at me
But all I know
To do to a man
Is to tell him just how it is
And let him do
Whatever he damn pleases about it
But I'll not beg
I won't beg nobody
I won't go a begging
I just ain't that lost.
I'm still a man
I can stand up and walk
I can walk and talk
And you can't stop me
You're crazy if you try it
You might want me to
Bow down here to you
But I won't beg you
I won't go a begging nobody.
A feller might give me some help
And I'd be much obliged
But I'll not beg you

I'll take it easy
But I'll dang shore take it.

I wrote this up one night looking for a home along the stem. It was in New York City during a right big snowy blizzard in February of nineteen and forty. I read it over in my old book here every few nights and it still sounds like I still feel about begging or asking for milk in my saucer like a cat.

I Don't Feel at Home on the Bowery No More

I'll sing you a song of the place that I stay
   Once on this Bowery I use to be gay
   Carefree and rambling in days of yore
But I don't feel at home on the Bowery no more

The flops they are lousy, the men are so thick,
   You can't go to sleep and you can't sleep a wink
   They mumble and grumble, they snarl and they snore
I don't feel at home on the Bowery no more.

The beds are so small that your feet touch the wall
   The bedbugs so big that they swallow you whole
   The lice are so thick that they cover the floor
I don't feel at home on the Bowery no more.

I seen an apartment on Fifth Avenue
   A penthouse and garden with a skyscraper view
   The carpets so soft with a hardwood floor
So I don't feel at home on the Bowery no more.

I like my good whiskey, I like my good wine,
   And good-looking women to have a good time

Cocktail parties and a big built-in bar
So I don't feel at home on the Bowery no more.

The girls on the Bowery have all advanced
    They're dancing for nickels at the old ticket dance
    I like pretty gals as I told you before
So I don't feel at home on the Bowery no more.

I got disgusted and I wrote this song
    I may be right and I may be wrong
    But since I seen the difference 'tween rich and the poor
I don't feel at home on the Bowery no more.

Written February eighteenth of nineteen-forty in the City
of New York, on West Fifty-Sixth Street, in Will Geer's house
in the charge of his wine and in the shadow of his kindness.
With a good thought for Herta Geer and Katie, Katie is about
seven months old, redheaded, husky, pretty like a picture.
Herta is older than that. She's the mama. And pretty like another picture. I dedicate this song to the Geer family and
to the bum situation up and down every Skid Row and
Bowery Street in this country. This bum situation is a big
situation. And since I wrote this song up, another third Geer
has been added, her name is Ella Geer, and this song is just as
much Ella's as it is any of the other Geers. This makes a song
with four Geers forward and none backward.

Build Me a World

Build me some ships that go a little faster
Build me some trains that get home quicker
Build me some cars that do things better
And build some planes that get you higher sooner.
Go take your tools
And take your books and work

And make the whole world over new again
This old one's served its time in balls and chains
Go take your tools and build our new world free.
Build me some houses where bugs can't eat the people
And put up buildings not full of disease
Invent milk wagons that stop at every door
And work out a Victory Garden for each hand
You want to build you say you want to build
You want to work you say you want to work
You want to study and you want to learn
Well go and build a world with honest wages
Build gambling games that will build orphans' homes
Build race tracks and raise horses that will run
And give the money to pregnant mothers' funds
Build me some factories where all colors meet
Build me some streets beat down by every color of feet
Build me some lawns and parks and yards that welcome all
And build me up some radio stations that talk sense
Can you build me some movies that have brains
Can you make me some mines that dig themselves
Can't you work out a tree to shade all men
Can't you put together a hoe that'll dig free dirt
And while you're building build me up a land
That finds each drop of sweat a useful place
Biuld me some mountains up to match my men
Build me a human world and a union race.

At Sea July 19, 1944
SS Sea Porpoise

Careless Reckless Love

Love, oh, careless reckless love
Love, oh, careless reckless love

It's love, oh, careless reckless love
There's nothin' in this world that it won't do

I was good to you and lovin' all the time
I was good to you and lovin' all the time
Good to you and loved you all of my good time
But still you never would be mine

You took away my silver and my gold
You took away my silver and my gold
You took away my silver and you took away my gold
But you shore cain't take away my soul

My heart is sad with a muddy old mind
My heart is sad with a muddy old mind
My heart is running muddy got trouble rising high
That one I want to love just won't be mine

I stand here alone in my back door
I stand here alone in my back door
I stand here alone in my back door
That's something I just never did do before

Thank your guiding stars above
Yes, thank your guiding stars above
Oh, thank your good guiding stars way up above
If you are free from careless reckless love

Love is one funny thing. Of all of the things I reckon love
is the funniest. You see, love is like a loaf of bread and you are
a part of the loaf. You're the baking powders and I'll show
you how. It takes you right up off the earth like a chunk of
chemicals. It beats you up, breaks you up in little pieces and
grinds you up to a fine powder between the rocks, then you
get powdered and ready to go on to get throwed and sifted
into the wind till the most of you has blowed to the four
corners of the earth and only the finest part of you remains.
Just whenever you think you've lost everything the oddest
actions of love's baking powders sets in and you see yourself

raised and lifted up feeling like a new man or like a new
woman. It's like that old song that shivers up and down my
back that goes, Since my sweetie has got to be an iceman, all
I get is the cold shoulder.

Here's a Tale a Feller Told Me

Here's a tale a feller told me
'Bout a kid he knowed back somewhere
Got in a hell of a lot of trouble,
Always was a pretty good kid, too.
 Seems like to me he was mulatto,
 Or some other Negro mixture,
 Heard his mom tell tales of the Ebo
 Land in Africa they'd sprung from.
Slave ships weighted down with lock-irons,
Black folks loaded in like sea fish,
Hundreds, thousands of them smothering
Down in the hull of an ocean sail ship.
 Black snake whips cracked by the ship's boss,
 Blistered hide and all-night groanings,
 How they all held their breath to save the
 Fresh air needed to stay alive on.
 Heads cracked up against the iron bolts
 Squirming bodies men and women,
 Slick and wet with sweat and blood that
 Trickled down on the slaves below them.
 Faces by the hundred thousands,
 Souls just bright as yours or mine is,
 Walked the gangplank to the mud bank
 All along the shores of freedom.

Chained around and tied together,
With their hands wired on their backsides,
She told stories how her papa
Come to the freedom land he'd heard about.
    Waded muddy roads and rocky
    Trails that wound across the swamplands,
    Stung and felt their blood run fever
    From the sleep-flies and mosquitoes.
        Worked in lines of new-born cotton
        Stalks neck high to the tallest field hand,
        Gritted their teeth and held their jaw square
        When the field boss cracked his long whip.
        Sick ones fell along the furrows
        Hungry ones fell out on the end rows,
        Cowards shook and turned to ashes;
        Brave ones kept the black race working.
            Graves are thick but tombstones never
            Seen along these watery lowlands
            Where the weak ones sleep beneath
            The crackling twigs the strong ones walk
                                                on.
                Lovers loved and word was marriage
                For the boss would not allow his
                Slaves to marry down on paper
                And they didn't have names to write
                                                there.

So,
This kid worked in a factory
Where they made some pretty bottles,
And one day he slung a quart one
Cracked up close to the floor boss' shoulder.
    And the floor boss grabbed a long whip
    Frailed the kid against a window

And the kid he grabbed the long whip,
And give the boss such an overhauling
That the sheriff and his men got called in, took the kid down
to the jail house and a lynch-mob come and got him and
they hung him on the river where that bridge bends over
yonder on that long iron hanging down there.

I Still Say to My Kid

I still say to my kid, and to my kids,
   you watched your mommy and your daddy have a big
   argument this morning, and you listened to your dad
   and mom rail and yell and shake their fists in the room
   at each other,
But, you, you kids, you boys, you girls, come on and keep
   growing.
Grow up faster and prettier than any of these wild flowers
   I've got growing out here in my back yard.
That's the way you'd ought to grow.
Just exactly like that little old green bushy tree out here that
   jumped out so full of leaves in these past few days.
Don't be little old kids all of your life till you grow big,
   and then, when you do get bigger, and as grown as you'll
   ever get, then's the right time to turn around and live
   like a kid again.

Me, and today,
Today here I'm awful worried and whipped up,
   I'm whipped up, but I'm not whipped down. And ten
   years from this day I'll still not be whipped down, no

matter how loud your mamma and me get and throw
things at each other.

No matter if you do see us older folks pulling crazy goofy
stunts, I still say to my kid,
                              Keep on a coming when you
                              feel like it.

Keep on and up and out and come.

May 30, 1948
Coney Island, N.Y.

Something Wrong

I have traveled around this land enough to know there's
something wrong
And I aim to try to fix it if I can and I think I can
Yes, I'm aiming to try to fix it and I think I can.
   I think I can and I think I can and I will die like a natural
man but I sure want to try to fix it if I can.
   Rich folks waste more than us poor could use and most
feet never tasted new shoes
   And I sure aim to try to fix things if I can and I think I can
   Yes, I sure aim to do some fixing and I think I can.

June 3, 1947
Coney Island, N.Y.

To a Young Negro Couple

I say to that young Negro boy and girl walking down here
along High Street, I see you laff and joke along here in the

dark, and you see me up here on the top step of this Oheb Shalam church.

I'm not up here to rain down any more meanness on your heap. No. I like to see you laff along on each other's shoulders. You walk just like you owned High Street, like Newark was your back yard. I watch you and wish you more goofy fun and funny laffs.

I give you High Street to goof around on. I hand you Newark to walk on laffing. You act so free and easy that I see in your walk a new kind of a gait coming. I hear in your jokey laff a better poem on its way.

You are the new poem of my up and coming walkers. I'll toss you all of this tonight.

April 4, 1948
Newark, New Jersey

Chorea and Me

I got my first good early look at my chorea on back several years ago as I watched how it worked on my mother, Nora Belle Guthrie, back in my old homey town of Okemah, Oklahoma.

I got myself such a good clear look at it (chorea) that I want to try to show you what things it caused her to do and how I fell heir to it through her.

I'm still glad I did fall heir to my chorea because it makes me stay dizzy and drunk all the time without guzzling down [illegible] or without paying my bartender one little blue cent.

It's been a couple or three good years ago when I herded my own rambling self in here to the door of my good Brooklyn State Hopeystial and give myself up to be looked at, observed, examined, checked over, digested, analyzed and scoreboarded from my head on down to try to see if I could find out and see what makes me walk around so dizzy as I do.

And just what it's been that makes me walk around dizzier every day, I stumbled in here just one hop ahead of it, but when you told me how it was that my mother passed it on to me, I guessed I'd better go on back towards old Okemah town one more time and try to tell you how I seen it hit her away on back before I even knew what name you called it by.

Some of you experts called it by one name and some of you called it by some other moniker. I just saw how odd it made her act and do around our house and I seen her lots more every day than my Dad ever seen her. He'd get up all bright and real early every morning and he'd nibble down his little bit of a breakfast and he'd go saddle up his horse and he'd ride on off to his office down in town, then she'd throw all of our furniture and all of our fixings, our chairs and our tables and our beds and our bookcases and our dressers all around over our whole house while she had one of her bad spells, and after her fit had worn itself off and gone on and left her, us kids would all go and pitch in and we'd help her straighten our whole place up again and get it all fixed up, nice and pretty again, by the time we heard Papa's foot heels scrape on our front porch for our suppertime.

I could see my mother get worser and worser every little passing minute of all my passing years even before I saw her get bad enuff, really bad enuff for any of my next door neighbors to get wind of what she done or even for my very own Daddy to get very wise to it all. I learnt how if not why it is that my people spend about a good ninety-nine and nine tenths of their earthly hours here on my worldly planet just trying to hide the simple little facts and truth of life from one another.

No Help Known

Huntington's Chorea
Means there's no help known
In the science of medicine
For me
And all of you Choreanites like me
Because all of my good nurses
And all of my good medicine men
And all of my good attenders
All look at me and say
By your words or by your looks
Or maybe by your whispers
There's just not no hope
Nor not no treatments known
To cure me of my dizzy [illegible]
Called Chorea
Maybe Jesus can think
Up a cure of some kind.

November, 1954
Brooklyn State Hospital

So Long, It's Been Good to Know You

I got the news that the war had begun
It was straight for the Army Hall that I run
And all of the people in my home town
Was a running up and a running down singing:

[248]

Chorus: So long, it's been good to know you
          So long, it's been good to know you
          So long, it's been good to know you
          There's a mighty big war that's got to be won
          And we'll get back together again.

The crowd was packed by the railroad track
People was yelling and patting my back
And while the engineer rung his bell
I hugged all the mothers and kissed all the gals, singing:

(Chorus)

I got to the camp and I learnt how to fight
Fascists in daytime, mosquitoes at night
I got my order to cross o'er the sea
So I waved "goodbye" to the girls I could see, singing:

(Chorus)

I got on a boat and I started to float
My old pack-sack and my big wool coat
With ten thousand men we rode the foam
And sung this song to the people back home:

(Chorus)

I landed somewhere on a fighting shore
With ten million soldiers and ten million more
And while we were chasing that Super Race
We sung this song in the chase. It was:

(Chorus)

So it won't be long till the fascists are gone
And all of their likes are finished and done
We'll throw the clods of dirt in their face
And walk away from that lonesome place singing:

(Chorus)

Made up on November 10, 1942

woody guthrie